Usborne Spotter's Guides
DINOSAURS

David Norman

Sedgwick Muse

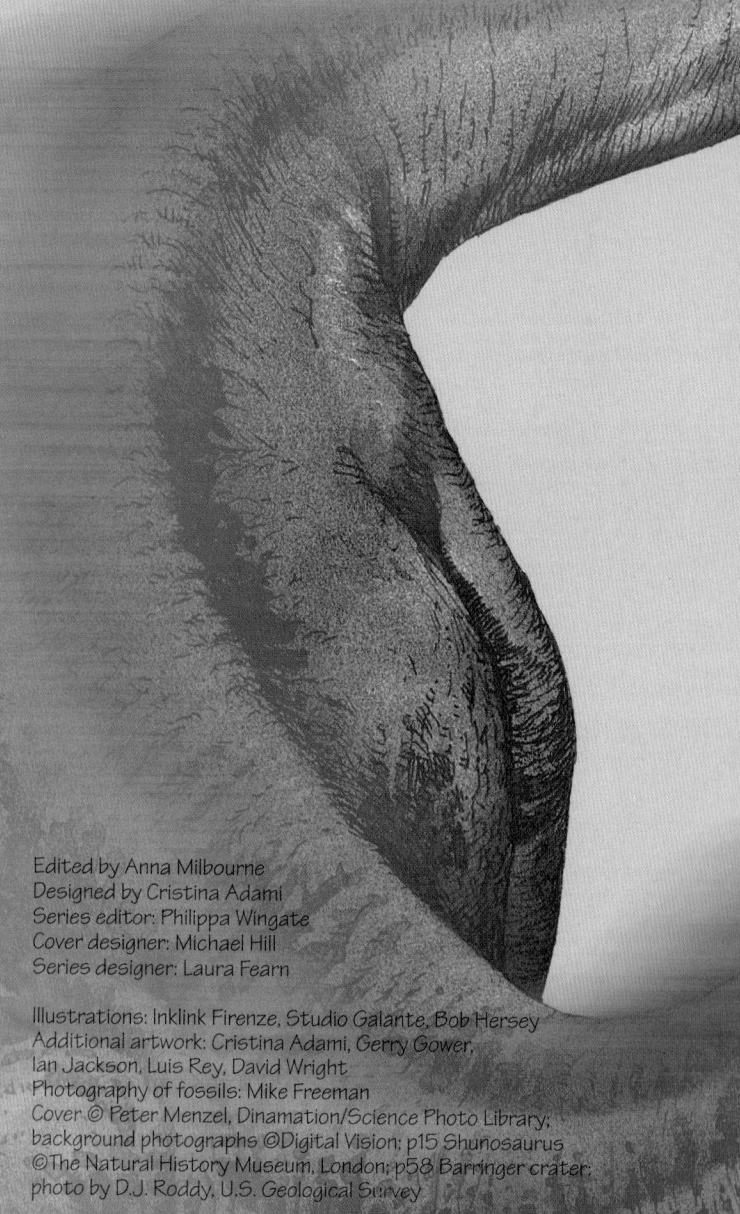

Edited by Anna Milbourne
Designed by Cristina Adami
Series editor: Philippa Wingate
Cover designer: Michael Hill
Series designer: Laura Fearn

Illustrations: Inklink Firenze, Studio Galante, Bob Hersey
Additional artwork: Cristina Adami, Gerry Gower,
Ian Jackson, Luis Rey, David Wright
Photography of fossils: Mike Freeman
Cover © Peter Menzel, Dinamation/Science Photo Library;
background photographs ©Digital Vision; p15 Shunosaurus
©The Natural History Museum, London; p58 Barringer crater:
photo by D.J. Roddy, U.S. Geological Survey

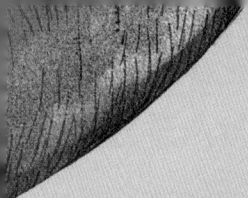

CONTENTS

HOW TO USE THIS BOOK

Dinosaurs are animals that are now extinct, which means they have all died out. This book is a guide to dinosaurs and other animals that lived millions of years ago. There are many museums you can visit to see dinosaur skeletons that scientists have found. Take this book with you if you go to a museum – it will help you imagine what these animals were like when they were alive.

PICTURES OF PREHISTORIC ANIMALS

The pictures in this book are based on the evidence scientists have found. They can learn a lot about a dinosaur by piecing together its remains to make a whole skeleton. They can work out its shape, how it moved and whether it walked on two legs or four. They can tell from its teeth whether it ate meat or plants. The only thing they cannot tell is the shade of a dinosaur's skin; so the skin shades in this book are imaginary.

PREHISTORIC ANIMAL NAMES

Many dinosaurs and other animals from this time have names ending in -*saurus*. This is a Greek word meaning *lizard*. It has been translated here as *reptile*, as this is closer to the truth. You can find out more about the group of animals to which dinosaurs and other prehistoric animals belong on page 8.

Dinosaurs have scientific names that describe them. For example, Velociraptor means *speedy reptile*. Under each scientific name, its meaning is shown in *italic* text. There is a guide under each name to help you say it. For example, (Tee-lee-oh-saw-rus). Emphasize the parts that are underlined.

5

TIME SCALE

Each animal description shows a time scale like the one below. The shaded area shows when the animal lived. Scientists have divided time since Earth began into four eras. Each era is divided into periods. Dinosaurs lived between 225 and 65 million years ago in the Mesozoic era. This era is divided into three periods – Triassic, Jurassic and Cretaceous.

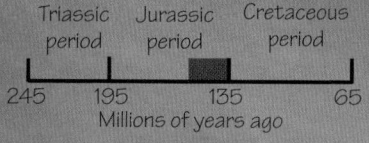

Triassic period | Jurassic period | Cretaceous period

245   195   135   65
Millions of years ago

PLACES

At the end of each animal description is the name of one or more countries or continents. This tells you where the remains of each animal have been found.

SIZE AND SHAPE

Each dinosaur or prehistoric animal in this book is measured from its head, down its backbone to the end of its tail. This measurement is known as the body length (BL).

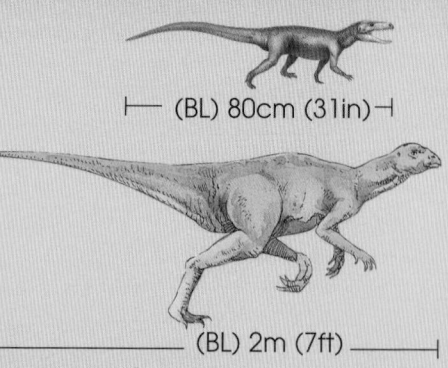

⊢— (BL) 80cm (31in) —⊣

⊢————— (BL) 2m (7ft) —————⊣

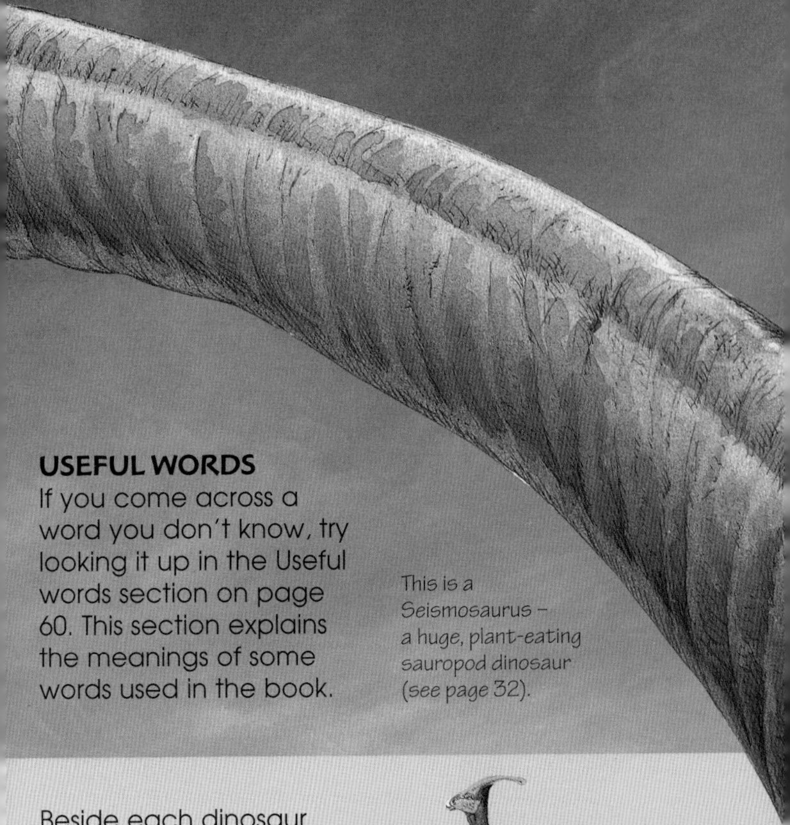

USEFUL WORDS

If you come across a word you don't know, try looking it up in the Useful words section on page 60. This section explains the meanings of some words used in the book.

This is a Seismosaurus – a huge, plant-eating sauropod dinosaur (see page 32).

Beside each dinosaur or prehistoric animal throughout the book you will find a small silhouette picture. This shows you roughly how big each animal would be compared to a person. Really small animals are compared to a person's hand.

7

For a link to a site where you can play dinosaur quizzes, turn to page 61.

WHAT ARE DINOSAURS?

A dinosaur is a type of reptile, although not the same as reptiles that are alive today. Dinosaurs belong to a group of animals called archosaurs. This group includes creatures that are well-known to us today, such as crocodiles and birds, as well as animals that are extinct, such as flying reptiles called pterosaurs. They all lay hard-shelled eggs and have scaly or feathered skin.

Archosaurs

All of these creatures are types of archosaurs.

Birds

Pterosaurs

Dinosaurs

Crocodiles

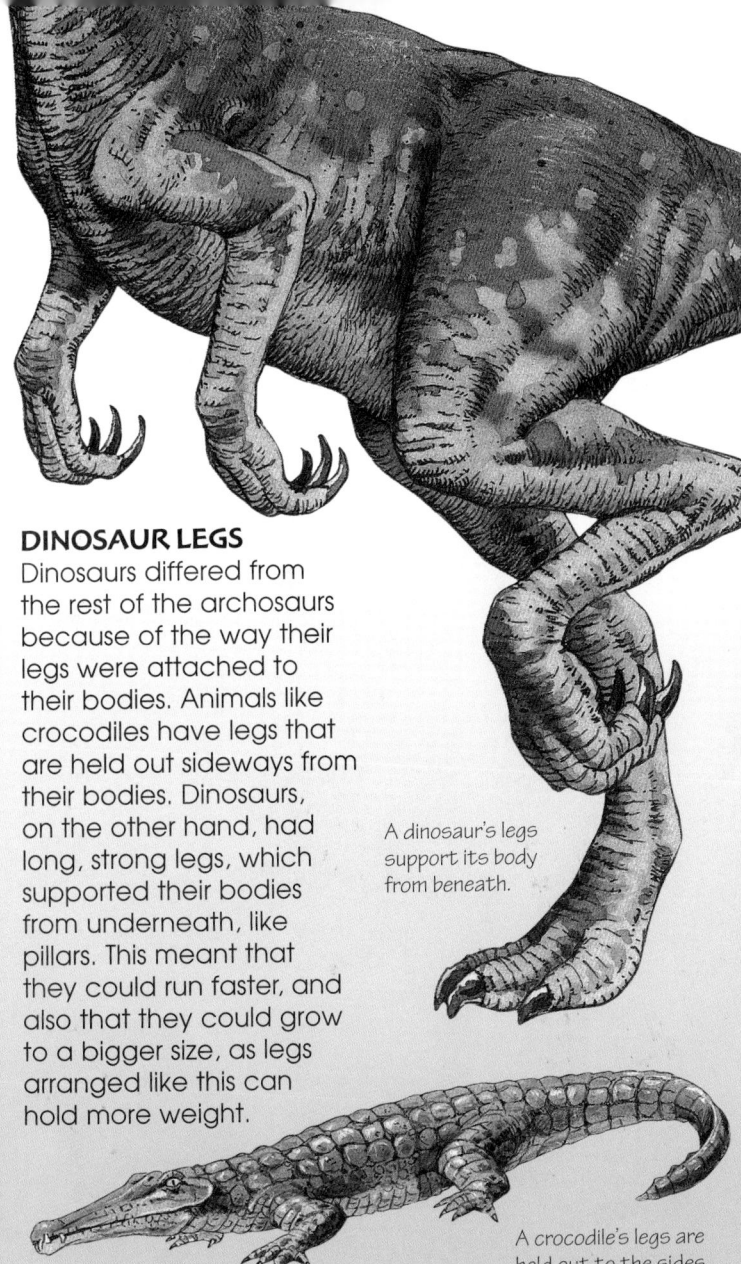

DINOSAUR LEGS

Dinosaurs differed from the rest of the archosaurs because of the way their legs were attached to their bodies. Animals like crocodiles have legs that are held out sideways from their bodies. Dinosaurs, on the other hand, had long, strong legs, which supported their bodies from underneath, like pillars. This meant that they could run faster, and also that they could grow to a bigger size, as legs arranged like this can hold more weight.

A dinosaur's legs support its body from beneath.

A crocodile's legs are held out to the sides.

9

TWO TYPES OF DINOSAURS

Dinosaurs are divided into two groups according to the shape of their hip bones. Dinosaurs are either "reptile-hipped" (called Saurischia), which means they had hips shaped like those of reptiles, or they are "bird-hipped" (called Ornithischia), which means they had hips shaped like those of birds. Strangely, birds today are related to reptile-hipped, not bird-hipped dinosaurs.

Apatosaurus – a type of sauropod.

Plateosaurus – a type of prosauropod.

Tarbosaurus – a type of theropod.

Pentaceratops – a type of ceratopian.

Scelidosaurus – a type of ankylosaur.

Reptile-hipped dinosaurs

REPTILE-HIPPED

There were two main kinds of reptile-hipped dinosaurs – huge plant-eaters which walked on all fours (called **sauropods** and **prosauropods**) and meat-eaters which walked on two legs (called **theropods**).

BIRD-HIPPED

Bird-hipped dinosaurs were all plant-eaters. There were two-legged **ornithopods**, duck-billed dinosaurs (**hadrosaurs**), dome-headed dinosaurs (**pachycephalosaurs**), horned dinosaurs (**ceratopians**), plated dinosaurs (**stegosaurs**), and armoured dinosaurs (**ankylosaurs**).

Iguanodon – a type of ornithopod.

Parasaurolophus – a type of hadrosaur.

Stegosaurus – a type of stegosaur.

Stegoceras – a type of pachycephalosaur.

Bird-hipped dinosaurs

TIME CHART

Era	Years ago (million)	Period	Climate
Mesozoic	65		Cool/variable
	135	Cretaceous	Warm/dry
	195	Jurassic	Warm/dry
	245	Triassic	Hot/dry
Paleozoic	280	Permian	Warm/dry / Cool
	345	Carboniferous	Glacial at South Pole / Tropical
	395	Devonian	Warm/dry
	440	Silurian	Warm
	500	Ordovician	Cool/warm
	570	Cambrian	Cold

This chart shows how scientists have split time into eras and periods, and when some prehistoric animals lived.

Ornithomimus   Tyrannosaurus   Pinacosaurus   Triceratops   Corythosaurus
Pachycephalosaurus   Pteranodon
Deinonychus   Protoceratops   Iguanodon

Ceratosaurus   Brachiosaurus   Stegosaurus   Rhamphorhynchus
Archaeopteryx   Compsognathus
Megazostrodon   Lesothosaurus   Scelidosaurus   Plesiosaurus
Coelophysis   Plateosaurus
Euparkeria   Mixosaurus
Proterosuchus

Dicynodon

Diplocaulus   Seymouria   Dimetrodon
Hylonomus

Ichthyostega
Eusthenopteron
Dunkleosteus   Cladoselache

Acabambaspis   Cup coral   Sea lily   Trilobite

Anomalocaris   Hallucigenia

13

For a link to a virtual tour of a dinosaur exhibition, turn to page 61.

WHAT ARE FOSSILS?

Fossils are the shapes or remains of animals and plants, preserved in rocks. Everything we know about dinosaurs is based on the study of their fossils.

HOW FOSSILS ARE FORMED

When animals die, their remains usually decay or are eaten. Fossils only form if the remains are quickly covered with sand or mud before this can happen. Over years, the mud or sand is compressed and turns into rock. The body of the animal decays, but the bones of the animal contain very tiny spaces, which gradually fill with minerals. This turns them (partly or wholly) into stone. Occasionally, the body of an animal or plant can be preserved without being turned into stone.

1. Millions of years ago an animal died and fell into the sea.

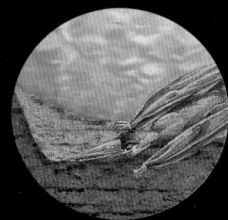

2. Its body sank to the sea bed, was covered in sand, and decayed.

RARE REMAINS

Very rarely, other sorts of remains can be preserved. These might be teeth, eggs, footprint tracks, impressions of skin or even droppings.

3. Minerals filtered into the animal's bones and turned them into stone.

This is the fossil skeleton of a dinosaur called Shunosaurus. It was found in China.

FINDING FOSSILS

When the rock surface wears away, fossils can be uncovered. Fossilized bones can be dug out of the rock and pieced together to show what an animal looked like.

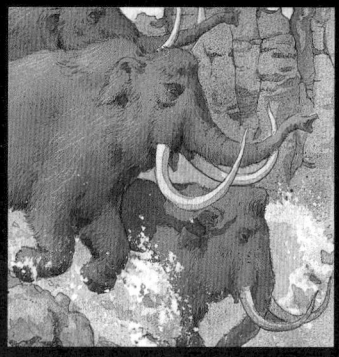

Remains of animals that have become extinct have also been found preserved in things other than rocks. In northern Siberia, mammoths have been found preserved in ice. The ice acted like a giant freezer.

15

For a link to a site about exciting dinosaur discoveries, turn to page 61.

CHANGING PLANET

The continents of the Earth may seem firm and solid but in fact they are moving very slowly all the time. This movement is called Continental Drift.

This shows the movement of the Earth's surface.

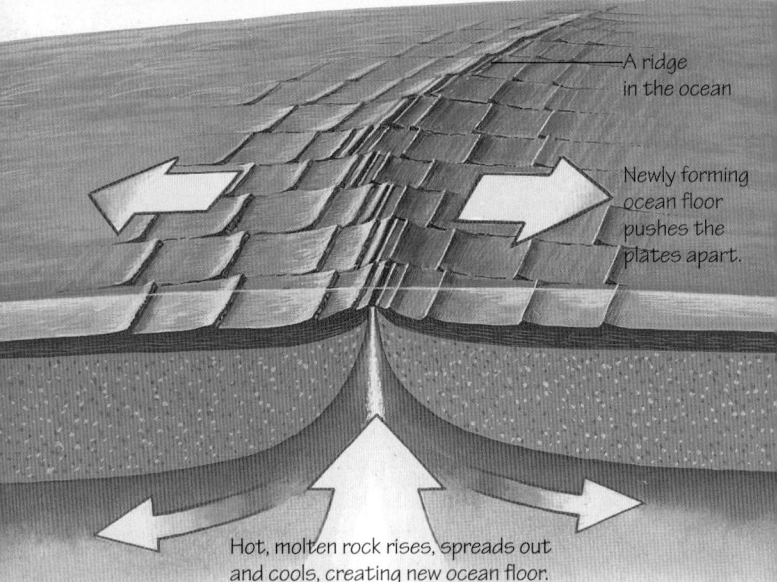

A ridge in the ocean

Newly forming ocean floor pushes the plates apart.

Hot, molten rock rises, spreads out and cools, creating new ocean floor.

The whole of the Earth's surface is divided up into giant sections, like a big jigsaw puzzle. These sections are called tectonic plates. Between the plates there are deep cracks (called trenches) and mountain ranges (called ridges).

At the ridges (either on the ocean floor or on land) molten rock rises from the core of the Earth. When it reaches the surface it cools and spreads out, forming new land or ocean floor. This pushes the plates outwards from the ridges.

This yellow line marks the position of a ridge in the ocean.

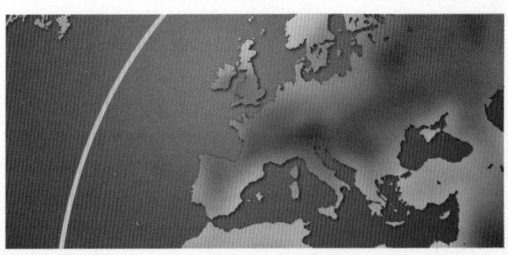

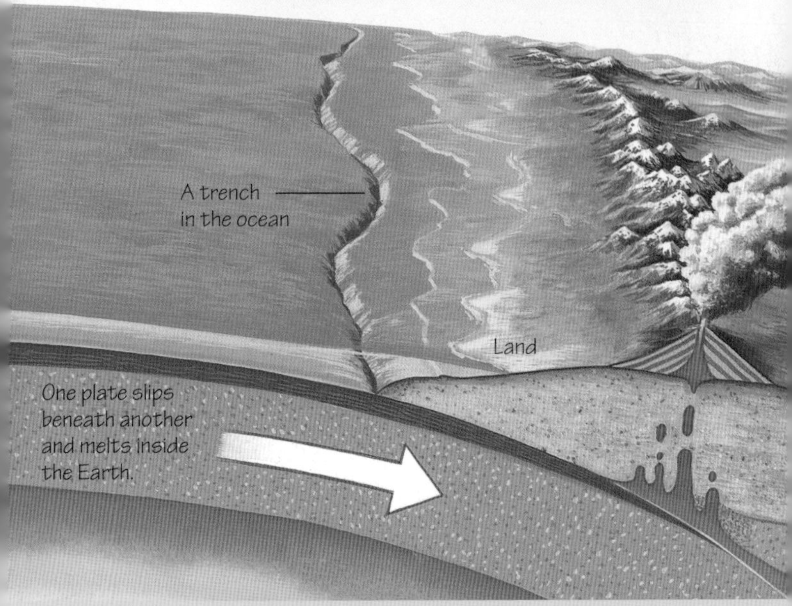

A trench in the ocean

Land

One plate slips beneath another and melts inside the Earth.

Since the Earth is not growing larger, there must also be areas where some of the ocean floor is disappearing. This happens at the trenches, where two tectonic plates are pushing against each other. One plate lifts and the other slips beneath it.

Over millions of years the continents have moved a long way. 200 million years ago, the coastlines of North and South America were joined to those of Africa and Europe. Since then, they have moved apart and are now separated by the Atlantic Ocean.

This shows how Earth has changed over millions of years.
Dinosaur fossils can be found on land that has moved
a long way since the dinosaurs were alive.

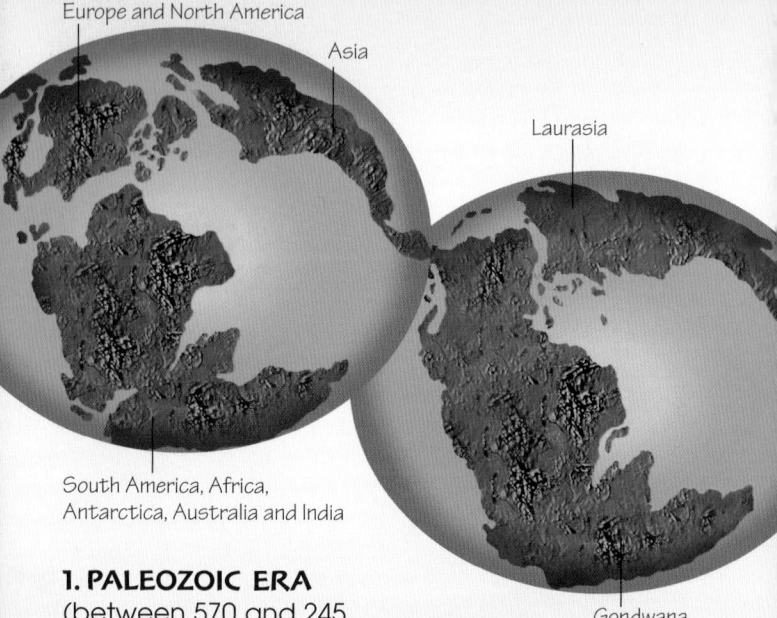

Europe and North America

Asia

Laurasia

South America, Africa,
Antarctica, Australia and India

Gondwana

1. PALEOZOIC ERA
(between 570 and 245
million years ago)

The movements of the
continents during this time
are not well known. There
seem to have been at
least three big continental
blocks – Europe and North
America, Asia, and a third,
made from all the other
continents (South America,
Africa, Antarctica,
Australia and India).

2. MESOZOIC ERA –
TRIASSIC PERIOD
(between 245 and 195
million years ago)

By this time, the three
continental blocks had
joined together to make
one huge continent
called Pangea. It had
two major parts – Laurasia
in the north and
Gondwana in the south.

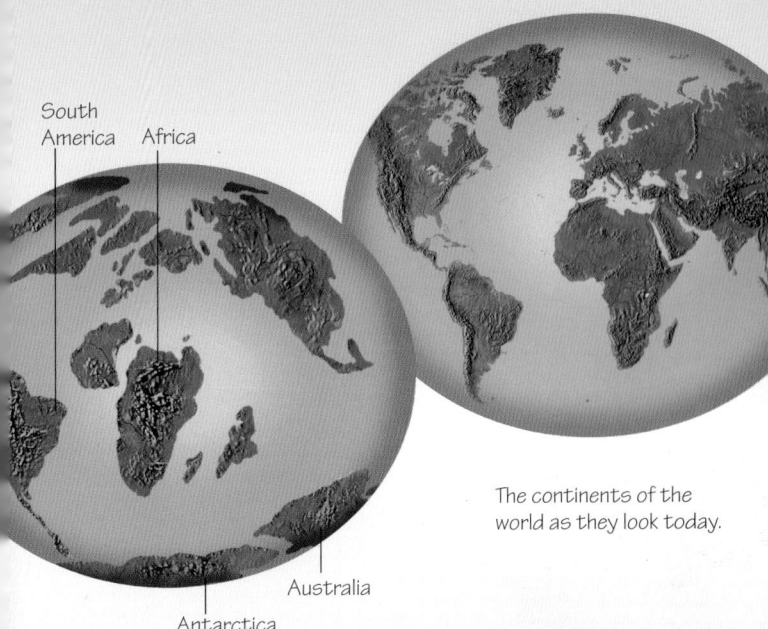

South
America Africa

Australia

Antarctica

The continents of the
world as they look today.

3. MESOZOIC ERA – CRETACEOUS PERIOD
(between 135 and 65 million years ago)

In the Jurassic period, Pangea had started to split up. Gondwana had begun to separate from Laurasia. By early Cretaceous times they were separate. By the end of the Cretaceous period, Gondwana was breaking into today's continents – South America, Africa, India, Antarctica and Australia.

4. RECENT TIMES
(between 65 million years ago and the present day)

The continental blocks continued to divide and separate from one another. Eventually they arrived in the positions they are in today. One of the last separations that took place was that between North America and Europe.

For a link to dinosaur digs and fossil discoveries, turn to page 61.

EARLY FOSSILS

➡ CAMBRIAN SCENE
These are some of the
earliest animals. Their fossils
were found in rocks called
the Burgess Shales in
western Canada, and
are about 530 million
years old. Some
animals look
like ancient
relatives of
animals
known today
– such as a
variety of
worms; others
are now extinct.

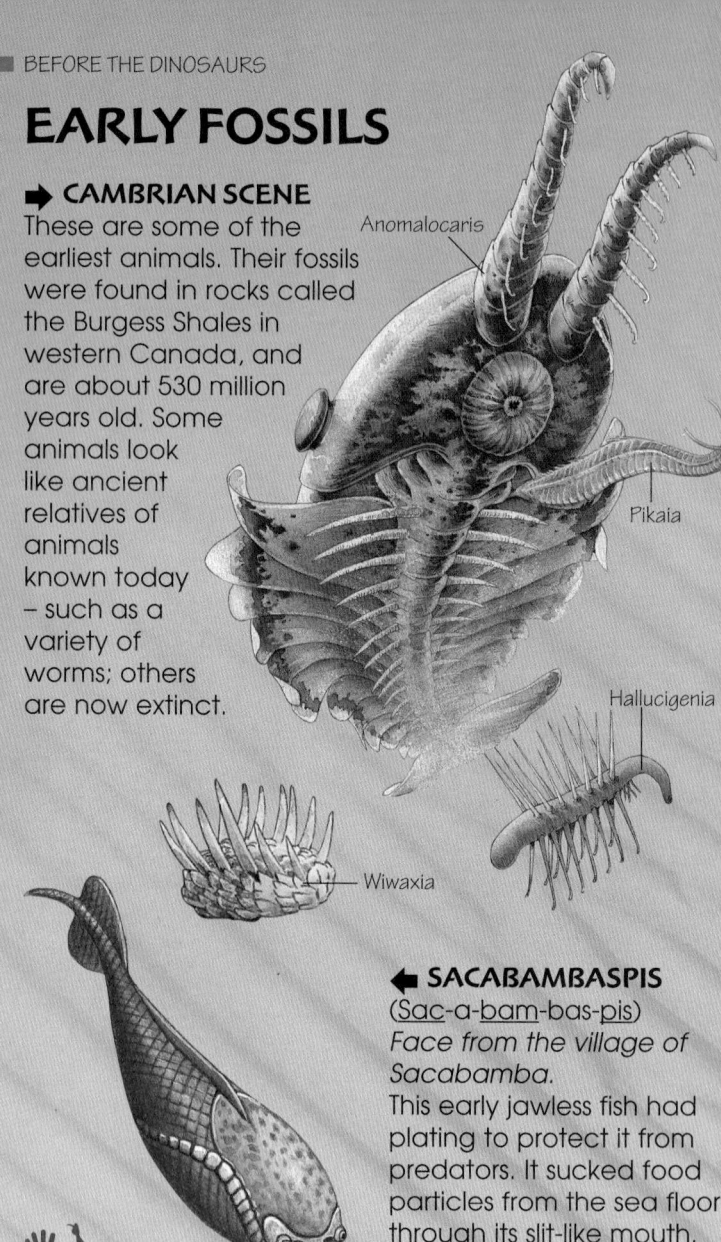

Anomalocaris

Pikaia

Hallucigenia

Wiwaxia

⬅ SACABAMBASPIS
(<u>Sac</u>-a-<u>bam</u>-bas-<u>pis</u>)
*Face from the village of
Sacabamba.*
This early jawless fish had
plating to protect it from
predators. It sucked food
particles from the sea floor
through its slit-like mouth.
Bolivia. BL 20cm (8in).

JAWED FISH

◄ DUNKLEOSTEUS
(Dun-kel-os-tee-us)
Dunkle's bones
The largest early fish with proper jaws. Its head alone was 3m (10ft) long. Having jaws meant that it could open its mouth wide. It ate other fish. USA. BL 10m (33ft).

➤ CLADOSELACHE
(Cla-doh-sell-ah-kee)
Ancestral shark
This early shark was similar to today's sharks, except for its large eyes and stiff fins and tail. USA. BL 1m (3ft).

◄ EUSTHENOPTERON
(Yews-then-op-tur-on)
True narrow fin
This bony freshwater fish had lungs as well as gills, so it could gulp air from the surface of shallow water. It used its strong fins to pull itself through weed-choked swamps. Greenland. BL 1m (3ft).

EARLY TETRAPODS

Any animal with four legs and a backbone is called a tetrapod. Early tetrapods were like today's amphibians – they could live on land and in water, and most laid their eggs in the water.

◄ ICHTHYOSTEGA
(Ik-thee-oh-<u>stee</u>-ga)
Fish roof
One of the earliest animals with legs and feet. It had a scaled, fish-like body and a tail fin. It used its front legs to hold its head out of the water to breathe. It could walk on land but spent most of its life in the water. It ate fish.
Greenland. BL 1m (3ft).

➤ DIPLOCAULUS
(Dip-lo-<u>cawl</u>-us)
Double stalk
This animal had a flattened body, small legs and a long tail for swimming. Its horns were probably used as stabilizers for swimming in fast-flowing streams. USA. BL 80cm (31in).

◄ SEYMOURIA
(See-<u>more</u>-ee-a)
From Seymour (Texas)
This animal's relatives laid eggs in the water, which hatched as tadpoles. It lived mainly on land. USA. BL 80cm (31in).

EARLY REPTILES

The early tetrapods developed into reptiles.
They could now lay hard-shelled eggs, which
did not dry out in the air. This meant that
they could live permanently on land.

➡ HYLONOMUS
(<u>Hie</u>-lo-<u>noh</u>-mus) *In-tree mouse*
One of the first reptiles. Its
body was lizard-like,
with scaly skin. It
ate insects.
Canada.
BL 10-20cm
(4-8in).

◄ DIMETRODON
(Die-<u>mee</u>-tro-don)
Two-sized tooth
This was a flesh-eater
with sharp teeth.
The "sail" on its
back helped
to control
its body
temperature.
USA. BL 3m (10ft).

➡ DICYNODON
(Die-<u>sine</u>-oh-don)
Two-dog tooth
This pig-shaped animal
was toothless, apart from
two tusks in its top jaw. It
ate plants. S. Africa.
BL 1m (3ft).

◄ LYCENOPS
(<u>Lie</u>-kay-nops) *Wolf-face*
This fierce flesh-eater had
a slim, scaly body, long legs
for chasing prey, and sharp
teeth. S. Africa. BL 1.5m (5ft).

23

EARLY ARCHOSAURS

The first archosaurs (see page 8) appeared in Permian times (about 260 million years ago). The first archosaurs were small, fast-moving animals with short backs, long necks and large heads with sharp, pointed teeth. Later, other archosaurs appeared, including animals like crocodiles, dinosaurs, pterosaurs and birds.

➡ PROTEROSUCHUS
(<u>Pro</u>-ter-oh-<u>soo</u>-<u>kus</u>)
Chasm reptile
A crocodile-like animal with a turned-down snout. It probably lived in water and ate fish. S. Africa. BL 2m (7ft).

⬅ EUPARKERIA
(<u>You</u>-park-<u>eer</u>-ee-a)
Parker's true reptile
Crocodile-like, but it was purely a land animal. It caught smaller prey and ate dead animals it found. S. Africa. BL 80cm (31in).

➡ ORNITHOSUCHUS
(<u>Or</u>-nith-oh-<u>sook</u>-us)
Bird-like crocodile
This flesh-eater ran on its back legs, leaving its arms free to catch prey. It was similar to the first dinosaurs. Britain. BL 3m (10ft).

SMALL THEROPODS

Theropods were meat-eating dinosaurs with strong back legs and grasping hands for catching prey. The small theropods tended also to be very agile, fast-moving animals with small heads and long necks.

← EORAPTOR
(Your-<u>apt</u>-or)
Dawn predator
An early dinosaur. It had big eyes for finding its prey, and hooked claws for killing it. Argentina. BL 2m (7ft).

➡ COMPSOGNATHUS
(Komp-sog-<u>nath</u>-us)
Pretty jaw
One of the smallest known dinosaurs. Fast-running meat-eaters such as this lived throughout the reign of the dinosaurs. Germany. BL 60cm (2ft).

➡ COELOPHYSIS
(See-low-<u>fi</u>-sis)
Hollow face
It had a slender body with hollow bones, making it light and agile. It was ferocious and probably fed on small, plant-eating dinosaurs. Mexico. BL 2m (7ft).

◀ COELURUS

(See-<u>lure</u>-us) *Hollow tail*
An agile meat-eater. It had long arms with sharp claws to catch prey. It may have fed on Compsognathus (page 25) and Archaeopteryx (page 52). Germany. BL 2m (7ft).

◀ VELOCIRAPTOR

(Vell-ossi-<u>rap</u>-tor)
Speedy predator
This animal ate reptiles and mammals. An unusual fossil was found of Velociraptor fighting Protoceratops (page 40) to the death. Mongolia. BL 1.5m (5ft).

▶ DEINONYCHUS

(Die-<u>non</u>-ee-kus)
Terrible claw
The fiercest, fastest flesh-eater. It leapt on prey, taking it by surprise and slashing with its large inner claw. It may have hunted in groups. USA. BL 2m (7ft).

26

LARGE THEROPODS

The largest theropods were a group called carnosaurs. Most carnosaurs had big heads, short necks and small arms. They killed their prey with their teeth or feet.

► DILOPHOSAURUS
(Die-<u>loaf</u>-oh-<u>saw</u>-rus)
Two-crested reptile
This was one of the earliest carnosaurs. It had long, powerful legs and short arms. No one knows why it had the two crests on its head. USA. BL 6m (20ft).

◄ ALLOSAURUS
(<u>Al</u>-oh-<u>saw</u>-rus)
Foreign reptile
This huge carnosaur hunted giant sauropods like Apatosaurus or Diplodocus (page 32). An Apatosaurus skeleton was found with Allosaurus toothmarks on it. N. America. BL 10m (33ft).

➡ SPINOSAURUS
(<u>Spine</u>-oh-<u>saw</u>-rus)
Spiny reptile
This unusual carnosaur had long spines (some up to 2m, or 7ft) forming a "sail" on its back. They helped to control its body temperature. Egypt. BL 8m (26ft).

⬅ MEGALOSAURUS
(<u>Mega</u>-low-<u>saw</u>-rus)
Giant reptile
This was the first dinosaur ever to be named and described (1824). England. BL 6m (20ft).

⬅ CERATOSAURUS
(Ser-<u>at</u>-oh-<u>saw</u>-rus)
Horned reptile
This carnosaur had a small horn on its head and bony ridges over its eyes. N. America. BL 6m (20ft).

➡ TYRANNOSAURUS
(Tie-ran-oh-saw-rus)
Tyrant reptile
One of the largest and last of the known theropods. It was taller than a giraffe, but was surprisingly light for its size. It tore its prey with its feet. Commonly known by its full name, Tyrannosaurus rex, this is the most famous meat-eater. USA. BL 15m (49ft).

Puny arms for its size

⬅ TARBOSAURUS
(Tar-bo-saw-rus)
Heroic reptile
This animal was similar to Tyrannosaurus. Many skeletons of this dinosaur have been found in recent years. Mongolia. BL 12m (39ft)

For a link to a site about the largest Tyrannosaurus fossil, turn to page 61.

STRANGE THEROPODS

A variety of theropods with unexpected features have been discovered. Some of these dinosaurs show similarities to today's birds. This is no coincidence, as birds and theropods are close relatives.

➡ ORNITHOMIMUS
(<u>Or</u>-nith-oh-<u>my</u>-mus)
Bird imitator
It had a beak but no teeth (rare for a meat-eater). It ate insects, dinosaur eggs, fruit and mammals.
N. America, Asia.
BL 3-4m (10-13ft).

⬅ THERIZINOSAURUS
(<u>Ther</u>-iz-<u>in</u>-oh-<u>saw</u>-us)
Scythe reptile
A strange-looking animal with a hairy body. It had a small head and small teeth, but huge claws on its front legs and powerful back legs.
Mongolia. BL 6m (20ft).

➡ OVIRAPTOR
(<u>Ov</u>-ih-<u>rap</u>-tor) *Egg robber*
An odd animal, with a big crest above its nose and a strong, sharp beak.
Mongolia. BL 2m (7ft).

PROSAUROPODS

Prosauropods were medium to large plant-eating dinosaurs that lived in late Triassic times. They have the same ancestors as the huge plant-eating sauropods of the Jurassic period (page 32).

➡ RIOJASAURUS
(<u>Ree</u>-ok-a-<u>saw</u>-rus)
Reptile from Rioja, Argentina
A bulky, heavy plant-eater.
It walked on all fours,
supporting its great weight
on massive, pillar-like legs
and powerful feet.
Argentina. BL 7m (23ft).

⬅ PLATEOSAURUS
(Plat-ee-oh-<u>saw</u>-rus)
Flat reptile
This animal lived in herds.
It walked on all fours, but
could stand on its back
legs to reach high leaves
on trees. It had small,
leaf-shaped teeth.
Germany. BL 6m (20ft).

SAUROPODS

Sauropods lived in Jurassic and Cretaceous times.
They had huge bodies, long necks and even longer
tails. They ate a wide range of plants, using their
peg-like teeth to strip leaves off trees. They
swallowed big stones to help crush up the
food in their stomachs.

➡ DIPLODOCUS
(Dip-lod-oh-kus)
Double beam
This dinosaur was very long,
with an extremely long tail,
which it used like a whip
to fend off enemies. It is
not the longest known
dinosaur, but one of the
most complete skeletons
yet found. N. America.
BL 27m (89ft).

➡ APATOSAURUS
(A-pat-oh-saw-rus)
Headless reptile
Used to be known as
Brontosaurus. Although
shorter than Diplodocus,
it was much heavier.
N. America. BL 20m (66ft).

For a link to a website where you can hear dinosaurs, turn to page 61.

➡ BRACHIOSAURUS
(Brack-ee-oh-<u>saw</u>-rus)
Arm reptile
It probably weighed the same as about seven elephants. Unlike other sauropods, its front legs were longer than its back ones, so it could reach the leaves on tall trees without having to stand on its back legs. Its nostrils were right on top of the bump on its head.
N. America. BL 23m (75ft).

33

ORNITHOPODS

Ornithopods walked mainly on their back legs. They had feet and hard beaks similar to those of birds. They were plant-eaters, and had cheeks to help contain their food when chewing.

← LESOTHOSAURUS
(Less-<u>oh</u>-toe-<u>saw</u>-rus)
Reptile from Lesotho
This was not a true ornithopod, as it had no cheeks, but it is closely related to all ornithopods. S. Africa. BL 90cm (35in).

← HETERODONTOSAURUS
(Het-er-oh-<u>don</u>-toe-<u>saw</u>-rus)
Mixed-tooth reptile
It was light and fast. It had tusks in its jaws to defend itself against enemies like Coelophysis (page 25). S. Africa. BL 90cm (35in).

→ HYPSILOPHODON
(Hip-see-<u>loaf</u>-oh-<u>don</u>)
High-ridged tooth
One of the fastest small dinosaurs. It used its stiff tail to balance when running. Britain, N. America. BL 2m (7ft).

34

← CAMPTOSAURUS
(Camp-toe-<u>saw</u>-rus)
Flexible reptile
This animal had claws on its hands and a pointed thumb spike. When chased, it ran on its back legs; when feeding on small shrubs, it moved on all fours. N. America, Britain. BL 5m (16ft).

→ IGUANODON
(Ig-<u>wa</u>-no-<u>don</u>)
Iguana tooth
It had very powerful back legs. A sharp claw on each thumb was probably used as a weapon against enemies. The other fingers had hooves, so it could walk on all fours. Europe, N. America. BL 10m (33ft).

DUCK-BILLED DINOSAURS

Duck-billed dinosaurs (or hadrosaurs) descended from animals like Iguanodon (page 35). They lived in late Cretaceous times. Their top jaw was flat at the tip, a little like a duck's bill. They had small, closely packed teeth for grinding tough, woody plants. Most duck-billed dinosaurs had similar bodies, but their heads were very different shapes.

◄ OURANOSAURUS

(Oo-ran-oh-saw-rus)
Valiant reptile
This dinosaur was related to the duck-bills, as it had a beak. However, it wasn't a true duck-bill. It had thumb spikes like Iguanodon. The spines on its back may have been supported by a hump (like a camel's), which helped control body temperature. Niger. BL 6m (20ft).

➤ EDMONTOSAURUS

(Ed-mon-toe-saw-rus)
Reptile from Edmonton
This duck-bill had four fingers on its hands (no thumb spikes). It lived in large herds for protection and ate a variety of plants. A surprisingly fast runner on its strong back legs. Canada.
BL 10m (33ft).

← KRITOSAURUS
(Krit-oh-<u>saw</u>-rus)
Noble lizard
This duck-bill had a flat head with a hump on its nose. This may have been used for butting rivals during the mating season. USA. BL 10m (33ft).

→ SAUROLOPHUS
(Saw-rol-<u>oh</u>-fus)
Ridged reptile
It had a prong on the back of its head. One suggestion is that this supported inflatable nose pouches so that the animal could bellow at rivals. N. America, Mongolia. BL10m (33ft).

← TSINTAOSAURUS
(<u>Sin</u>-ta-oh-<u>saw</u>-rus)
Reptile from Tsintao
Some scientists think it had a long spike on top of its head. This could have been used as a weapon, as well as to support its nose pouches. China. BL 10m (33ft).

← ANATOTITAN
(An-<u>a</u>-toe-<u>ti</u>-tan) *Big duck*
Thought to be one of the last dinosaurs, this duck-bill had a wide beak and probably made honking noises.
N. America. BL13m (43ft).

← CORYTHOSAURUS
(Ko-<u>rith</u>-oh-<u>saw</u>-rus)
Helmeted reptile
Passages inside this animal's crest may have helped it to make honking noises. Individuals of a herd recognized each other by their crest shapes.
N. America. BL 10m (33ft).

→ PARASAUROLOPHUS
(Para-<u>saw</u>-ro-<u>loh</u>-fus)
Reptile with parallel-sided crest
Its crest was hollow with air passages inside. These probably helped make its honking noises louder. N. America.
BL 10m (33ft).

DOME-HEADED DINOSAURS

Dome-headed dinosaurs (or pachycephalosaurs) were closely related to ornithopods (page 34). They had similar bodies and were also bird-hipped plant-eaters. However, the dome of their skulls was extraordinarily thick. They lived in late Cretaceous times.

➡ STEGOCERAS
(Steg-_oss_-er-ass)
Horn roof
Remains are rare, as it probably lived in the uplands, where few fossils are ever preserved. It is quite possible that it lived as mountain sheep do today. N. America, BL 3m (10ft).

➡ PACHYCEPHALOSAURUS
(Pack-ee-_sef_-al-oh-_saw_-rus)
Thick-headed reptile
The dome on its head was very thick and surrounded by bumps and spikes. Some scientists think they had head-butting contests; others think they used their domes to recognize one another. Canada. BL 8m (26ft).

39

For a link to a website with interactive dinosaur activities, turn to page 61.

HORNED DINOSAURS

These horned dinosaurs with parrot-like beaks are called ceratopians. They lived in late Cretaceous times. Most of them can be recognized by the shape of their horns or neck frill.

➡ PSITTACOSAURUS
(<u>Sit</u>-ak-oh-<u>saw</u>-rus)
Parrot reptile
It had a hooked beak on its top jaw. It walked on its back legs, ate plants and probably used its clawed hands for digging.
Mongolia. BL 2m (7ft).

⬅ PROTOCERATOPS
(<u>Pro</u>-toe-<u>ser</u>-a-tops)
First horned face
Had a big frill on the back of its head. Used its large, hooked beak for slicing leaves off tough plants.
Mongolia. BL 2m (7ft).

Nests of Proceratops' eggs were found, with fossil fragments of baby dinosaurs that had died before hatching. The eggs were found arranged in a circle. Mongolia.

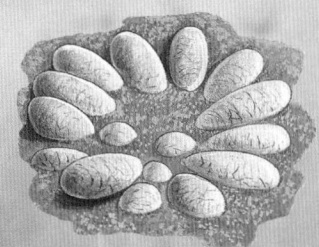

➡ **MONOCLONIUS**
(<u>Mon</u>-oh-<u>clo</u>-nee-us)
Single shoot
This animal looked similar
to a rhinoceros of today.
It had a single horn on its
nose, and small eyebrow
ridges. It lived in herds.
N. America. BL 8m (26ft).

⬇ **PENTACERATOPS**
(<u>Pent</u>-ah-<u>ser</u>-a-tops)
Five-horned face
Its large frill extended
halfway down its back.
Apart from its nose and
eyebrow horns, it had two
pointed cheekbones, like
horns, beneath its eyes.
N. America. BL 7m (23ft).

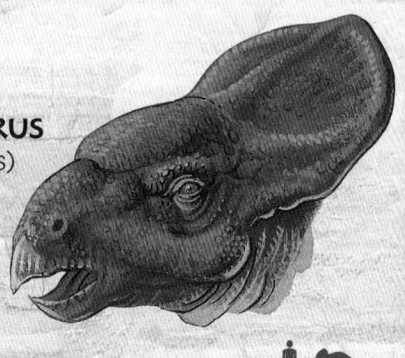

➡ PACHYRHINOSAURUS
(Pack-ee-<u>rye</u>-no-<u>saw</u>-rus)
Thick-nosed reptile
A hornless ceratopian
with a short frill. It had
thick bone on top of its
nose between its eyes.
Canada. BL 4m (13ft).

⬅ LEPTOCERATOPS
(<u>Lep</u>-toe-<u>ser</u>-a-tops)
Slender-horned face
An unusual, small
ceratopian that ran on its
back legs. Its frill was small
and it had no horns, as it
could run away from
predators, rather than
trying to defend itself.
N. America. BL 2m (7ft).

⬇ TRICERATOPS
(Try-<u>ser</u>-a-tops)
Three-horned face
The largest ceratopian
and one of the last. It was
about the same weight as
two elephants. N. America.
BL 11m (36ft).

42

PLATED DINOSAURS

Plated dinosaurs, or stegosaurs, were big plant-eaters whose remains have been found in rocks of Jurassic and early Cretaceous times as far apart as N. America, Europe, Africa and China. They can be easily recognized by the high, plate-like (or sometimes pointed) bones running in rows down their backs. Their tails ended in large, vicious-looking spines.

➡ KENTROSAURUS
(<u>Ken</u>-tro-<u>saw</u>-rus)
Prickly reptile
In danger, it would probably have turned its back on a predator. The spiky tail would have made attacking it difficult. Tanzania. BL 5m (16ft).

⬇ STEGOSAURUS
(<u>Steg</u>-oh-<u>saw</u>-rus)
Roofed reptile
The largest known stegosaur. It was thought that the plates on its back were for protection. Now experts believe that they were used for regulating body temperature. N. America. BL 8m (26ft).

ARMOURED DINOSAURS

These were medium to large, slow-moving plant-eaters. They are found through much of the dinosaur era – from the early Jurassic to the end of the Cretaceous period. They are called ankylosaurs (*fused reptiles*) because of their bony plating.

➡ SCELIDOSAURUS
(Skell-id-oh-saw-rus)
Limb reptile
One of the earliest armoured dinosaurs. It had a heavily plated back and head, and fed on plants.
England. BL 4m (13ft).

⬅ POLACANTHUS
(Poll-a-can-thus)
Many-spined
This dinosaur had shield-like plating over its hips and the top of its head. It also had many spines on its back. Isle of Wight. BL 4m (13ft).

➡ PINACOSAURUS
(Pee-nah-co-saw-rus)
Spiky reptile
Thick, flexible plates covered its head, neck, back and tail, protecting it against carnosaurs. Mongolia. BL 4.5m (15ft).

44

➡ EUOPLOCEPHALUS
(<u>Yew</u>-oh-plo-<u>sef</u>-al-us)
True-plated head
It had heavy, bony plating and lumps on its skin. Thick bone covered its head, like a helmet. Its belly was soft and unprotected. It probably used its tail like a club to defend itself.
N. America. BL 7m (23ft)

⬅ NODOSAURUS
(<u>Noh</u>-doh-<u>saw</u>-rus)
Lumpy reptile
It had bands of bony lumps across its back. These acted as protective plating. It does not seem to have had a tail club like other armoured dinosaurs.
N. America. BL 6m (20ft).

➡ PANOPLOSAURUS
(<u>Pan</u>-oh-plo-<u>saw</u>-rus)
All-armoured reptile
It had simple leaf-shaped teeth and its jaw ended in a hard, toothless beak. It had spikes along its sides and across the back of its neck.
N. America. BL 7m (23ft).

For a link to a website with dinosaur games and activities, turn to page 61.

FLYING REPTILES

Pterosaurs were light, fragile reptiles that flew. Their wings were leathery pieces of skin stretched along their long fourth finger. They seem to have evolved from early dinosaurs such as Eoraptor (see page 25).

➡ SHAROVIPTERYX
(Shah-roh-<u>vip</u>-tur-iks)
Sharov's wing
An early gliding reptile, similar to pterosaurs. It glided between branches using skin stretched between its tail and legs. Kazakhstan. BL 20cm (8in).

⬅ DIMORPHODON
(Die-<u>more</u>-foe-don)
Two types of tooth
One of the first pterosaurs. Its wing span was about 1m (3ft). Most of its wing was supported by its long end finger. England. BL 40cm (16in).

➡ RHAMPHORHYNCHUS
(<u>Ram</u>-foe-<u>rin</u>-kus)
Beak-nose
It swooped low over the sea, spearing fish with sharp, forward-pointing teeth. Its large eyes helped it to spot fish. Germany. BL 30cm (1ft).

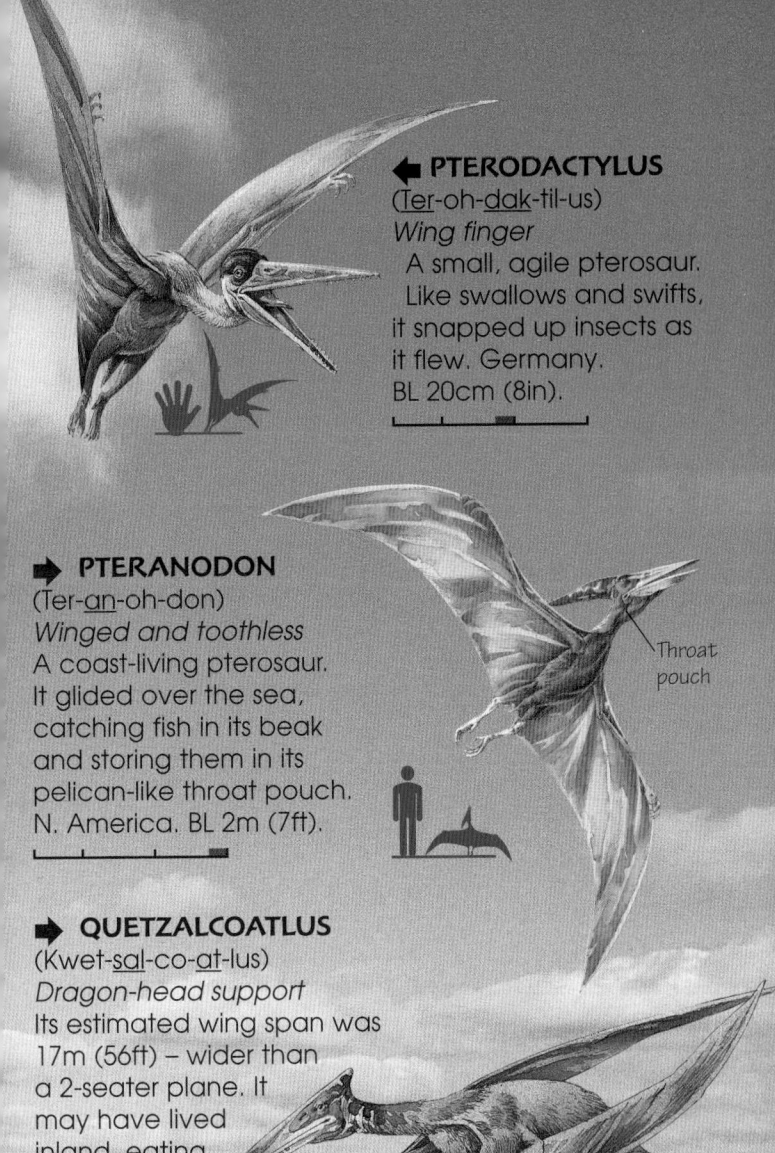

◄ PTERODACTYLUS
(<u>Ter</u>-oh-<u>dak</u>-til-us)
Wing finger
  A small, agile pterosaur.
  Like swallows and swifts,
it snapped up insects as
it flew. Germany.
BL 20cm (8in).

➡ PTERANODON
(Ter-<u>an</u>-oh-don)
Winged and toothless
A coast-living pterosaur.
It glided over the sea,
catching fish in its beak
and storing them in its
pelican-like throat pouch.
N. America. BL 2m (7ft).

Throat
pouch

➡ QUETZALCOATLUS
(Kwet-<u>sal</u>-co-<u>at</u>-lus)
Dragon-head support
Its estimated wing span was
17m (56ft) – wider than
a 2-seater plane. It
may have lived
inland, eating
dead animals.
N. America. BL unknown.

PHYTOSAURS AND CROCODILES

Phytosaurs were early, crocodile-like archosaurs that lived at the end of the Triassic period. Today's crocodiles and alligators are related to animals that lived millions of years ago, such as Protosuchus, an early crocodile. Unlike today's crocodiles, these early crocodiles lived mainly on land.

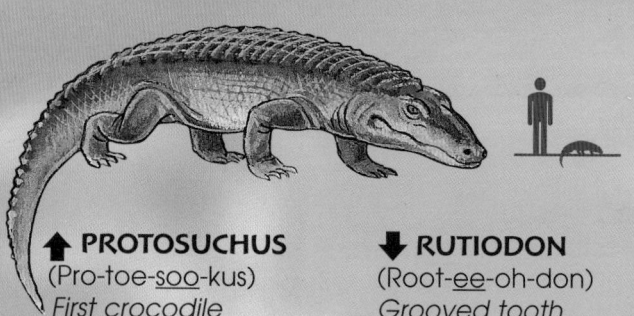

⬆ PROTOSUCHUS
(Pro-toe-soo-kus)
First crocodile
One of the earliest crocodiles. It had a short head and, for a crocodile, quite long legs. It fed on lizards and frogs. N. America. BL 1m (3ft).

⬇ RUTIODON
(Root-ee-oh-don)
Grooved tooth
This phytosaur was very like a crocodile, with its long body, powerful tail, bone-plated skin, long jaws and short, strong legs. Its nostrils were on a mound between its eyes. In true crocodiles, these are on the tip of the snout. Africa. BL 4-5m (13-16ft).

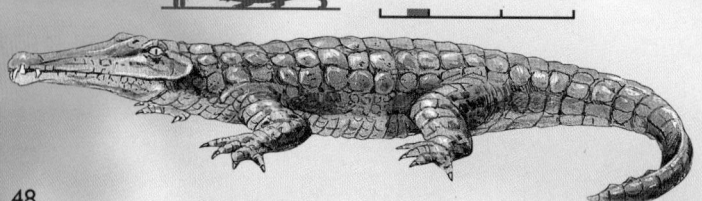

◀ METRIORHYNCHUS
(<u>Met</u>-ree-oh-<u>rin</u>-kus)
Long nose
It lived in the sea, unlike most crocodiles, which live in rivers. It had sharp teeth for catching fish, and swam using its tail and webbed feet. England. BL 4m (13ft).

◀ TELEOSAURUS
(<u>Tee</u>-lee-oh-<u>saw</u>-rus)
Tail reptile
This crocodile lived near estuaries and ate fish. It was not as good a swimmer as Metriorhynchus, as it had no tail flipper. Europe, Africa. BL 4m (13ft).

▶ BERNISSARTIA
(<u>Bur</u>-nee-<u>sar</u>-tee-ah)
Crocodile from Bernissartia
This crocodile's blunt teeth show it may have fed on shellfish or dead animals. Belgium, England. BL 60cm (2ft).

◀ DEINOSUCHUS
(<u>Die</u>-no-<u>soo</u>-kus)
Terrible crocodile
This crocodile's head was over 2m (7ft) long. So far, only its skull has been found. N. America. BL unknown.

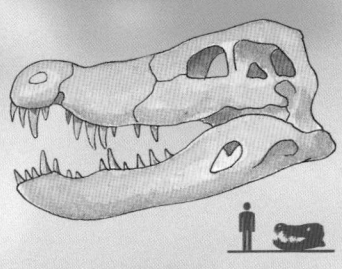

SWIMMING REPTILES

Several kinds of sea-dwelling animals lived in the Mesozoic era, at the same time as the dinosaurs. Ichthyosaurs looked similar to today's fish and dolphins. Plesiosaurs, pliosaurs and nothosaurs were less fish-like.

➡ MIXOSAURUS
(Mix-oh-saw-rus)
Mixed reptile
One of the first ichthyosaurs. Its tail had a fish-like fin and it used its legs as paddles. It had many sharp teeth for catching fish. Europe. BL 2-3m (7-10ft).

◀ ICHTHYOSAURUS
(Ik-thee-oh-saw-rus)
Fish reptile
This ichthyosaur's tail was like that of a fish. It swam by lashing its tail from side to side, and it balanced and steered with its flippers. Europe. BL 1-8m (3-26ft).

➡ OPHTHALMOSAURUS
(Off-thal-mow-saw-rus)
Eye reptile
An ichthyosaur with big eyes for seeing underwater. It ate squid-like animals whole, as it had no teeth. Europe. BL 4-5m (13-16ft).

➡ NOTHOSAURUS
(<u>No</u>-thow-<u>saw</u>-rus)
Southern reptile
This nothosaur lived in the sea, but came ashore to lay eggs. It caught fish with its sharp teeth. Europe, Asia, Africa. BL 3m (10ft).

➡ PLESIOSAURUS
(<u>Plees</u>-ee-oh-<u>saw</u>-rus)
Ribbon reptile
This plesiosaur swam slowly, flapping its flippers like a turtle. Fossilized stomach contents show that it ate squid-like creatures called belemnites as well as fish. Europe. BL 2-9m (7-30ft).

⬅ LIOPLEURODON
(<u>lie</u>-oh-<u>ploor</u>-oh-don)
Smooth-sided tooth
This was a ferocious pliosaur which ate large turtles, plesiosaurs and other sea reptiles. It swam by flapping its flippers. Australia. BL 13m (43ft).

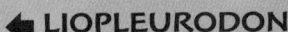

THE EARLIEST BIRD

New discoveries in China prove that birds are the living descendants of theropod dinosaurs. Some theropods had fluff or feathers covering their bodies. The first true bird was Archaeopteryx.

➡ ARCHAEOPTERYX
(Are-kee-op-tur-iks)
Ancient wing
This early bird may have had to climb trees to launch itself into the air. Today's birds evolved from this one. Europe. BL 20cm (8in).

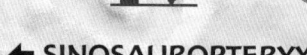

⬅ SINOSAUROPTERYX
(Sine-oh-saw-op-ter-iks)
Chinese reptile bird
This small dinosaur had fluff covering its body. It was similar to Compsognathus (page 25). China. BL 60cm (2ft).

⬅ CAUDIPTERYX
(Cor-dip-ter-iks) *Tail wing*
As well as having fluff on its body to keep it warm, this small dinosaur also had feathers on its tail and arms. It could not fly. China. BL 80cm (31in).

THE EARLIEST MAMMAL

Today's mammals are related to creatures like Dimetrodon (page 23) which lived before dinosaurs were alive. By the early Triassic period creatures that looked more mammal-like started to appear. They looked quite similar to dogs or rats.

◀ CYNOGNATHUS
(<u>Sine</u>-og-<u>nath</u>-us) *Dog jaw*
This wasn't a mammal, but looked like a dog. Like mammals, it had several different types of teeth (a reptile's teeth are usually all the same). Africa. BL 2m (7ft).

➡ THRINAXODON
(Thrin-<u>axe</u>-oh-don)
Trident tooth
This was not a mammal, but was even more mammal-like than Cynognathus. It had teeth of different kinds, whiskers on its nose, and was probably hairy like a mammal. S. Africa.
BL 40cm (16in).

◀ MEGAZOSTRODON
(<u>Meg</u>-ah-<u>zost</u>-ro-don)
Big girdle tooth
The earliest known mammal. It was hairy and gave birth to young. It was like a shrew and ate insects. S. Africa.
BL 6-8cm (2-3in).

FOSSILS

Fossils are hugely important in gathering information about prehistoric life. This section shows types of fossils that have been found.

➡ FOSSIL FERN

Fern fronds are often found in rocks from Carboniferous times. They are common plants of this period, often found alongside early tetrapods.

⬅ CUP CORAL

These early corals lived in cup-shaped limestone on the sea floor. They were the oldest coral animals, living before and right through the age of dinosaurs. Now they are replaced by reef corals.

➡ BRACHIOPODS

(<u>Brack</u>-ee-oh-pods)
Lampshells
These are common fossils, found in rocks from early Cambrian to recent times. Attached by a stalk to the sea bed, the shell housed an animal which filtered food from the water.

➡ GASTROPODS

Gastropods are animals with simple shells, like snails. They have been common since Cambrian times. The shells in which they lived were various shapes – coiled, spiral-shaped, or cone-shaped.

➡ BIVALVES

Bivalves have two shells hinged together, in which an animal lives (or lived). Cockles, mussels and razor shells are bivalves. Bivalves are very common fossils. In some cases, great lumps of rock are made entirely of broken bivalve shells.

⬅ AMMONITE

Ammonites were related to animals like snails and octopuses. Many ammonites lived in the sea until late Cretaceous times, then died out. The coiled shell contained chambers filled with air, which helped the animal to float.

➡ TRILOBITE
(<u>Try</u>-low-bite)
Three-lobed
Trilobites lived from Cambrian to Triassic times. They had hard shells and many, jointed legs. Most trilobites found food on the sea floor.

⬅ CRINOID
(<u>Crin</u>-oyd) *Sea lily*
Sea lilies are related to sea urchins and starfish. Attached to the sea floor by a stalk, they used their long tentacles to catch tiny bits of food (plankton) from the water.

➡ VERTEBRATE FOSSILS
Fossils of backboned animals that lived on land or in the air are rarer than those of sea animals. Sometimes a complete skeleton is discovered, but usually just an odd tooth or bone is found. These can be difficult to identify.

This is a fossil skeleton of Seymouria (page 22).

LIVING FOSSILS

Some modern-day animals look like living examples of prehistoric animals. Some have developed very little, and some have not changed since prehistoric times.

➡ TUATARA
This is a relative of lizard-like animals from Triassic times. It lives on islands near New Zealand. It looks nearly the same as its relatives did 200 million years ago.

⬅ PEARLY NAUTILUS
A rare, distant, living relative of squids, octopuses and extinct ammonites (page 55). It lives in a coiled shell which helps it to float in water. It is found in the Indian Ocean.

➡ COELACANTH
(see-la-canth)
Hollow spine
A big, predatory fish that lives in the Indian Ocean. It is closely related to Eusthenopteron (page 21).

➡ BRACHIOPODS
Brachiopods (also page 54) can be traced back to Cambrian times. An animal lives inside two hinged shells, which are attached to the sea floor by a stalk.

WHY DID THE DINOSAURS DIE OUT?

Fossil dinosaurs have been found in rocks from the Mesozoic era. But there are none in rocks that are newer than this. This shows that dinosaurs became extinct 65 million years ago, at the end of the Mesozoic era. Scientists think that dinosaurs died out because something violent suddenly changed the Earth's climate. Here are two explanations of what may have happened.

VOLCANIC THEORY

65 million years ago there were some huge volcanic eruptions in what is now India. Any animals close to the eruptions were killed immediately. Dust and gases from these volcanoes blocked out the sunlight and the world became cold and dark. Without sunlight all the plants died. The cold may have been enough to kill the dinosaurs, or they may have starved to death.

For a link to a site about different extinction theories, turn to page 61.

IMPACT THEORY

Many scientists think that a huge lump of rock from space, called an asteroid, hit the Earth. The asteroid was probably about 10km (6 miles) across. Yucatan in Mexico could be the place the asteroid hit, as a crater 200km (125 miles) wide has been found there. In the same way as described in the volcanic theory, vast clouds of dust and gas filled the air all around the world. Sunlight was blocked out so the Earth became cold, and plants then animals died.

This huge crater in Arizona was made by an asteroid hitting the Earth.

SURVIVORS

Many animals including birds, mammals, insects and sea creatures survived after the dinosaurs died out. Why some animals survived while others died is still a mystery.

USEFUL WORDS

This page explains some of the words used in the book. Words in *italic* text are explained separately.

amphibian – a backboned, usually four-legged animal that lays jelly-covered eggs in water. Examples include frogs and newts.

archosaur – a group of *reptiles* that includes crocodiles, birds, dinosaurs and pterosaurs.

descendant – an animal which is believed to have *evolved* from another animal.

evolution – the process by which many scientists believe types of plants and animals gradually, over millions of years, alter and become better suited to living in a particular environment.

extinct – died out. An animal is extinct if there are no animals of that type left alive.

fossil – the remains or impression of a dead plant or animal, preserved in rock.

mammal – a backboned, usually four-legged animal that gives birth to babies which are fed on their mother's milk. Examples include humans, mice, bats, horses and whales.

predator – an animal that kills and eats other animals.

prey – an animal that is hunted and killed by another animal.

prehistoric – before history started being written down by humans.

related – belongs to the same group of animals. For example, lions and tigers are related.

reptile – a backboned, usually four-legged animal which has a scaly skin and lays shelled eggs on land. Examples include lizards, snakes, tortoises, crocodiles, dinosaurs and pterosaurs.

tetrapod – any animal with four legs and a backbone.

INTERNET LINKS

If you have access to the Internet, you can visit these websites to find out more about dinosaurs. For links to these sites, go to the Usborne Quicklinks Website at **www.usborne-quicklinks.com** and enter the keywords "spotters dinosaurs".

Internet safety

When using the Internet, please follow the **Internet safety guidelines** shown on the Usborne Quicklinks Website.

WEBSITE 1 Watch dinosaur video clips, play games and even hear what dinosaurs may have sounded like.

WEBSITE 2 Find out about exciting dinosaur discoveries and unearth some fascinating facts about dinosaurs.

WEBSITE 3 Dig up dinosaur data, and find puzzles, tips for fossil-hunting, and theories about why dinosaurs became extinct.

WEBSITE 4 Links to dinosaur games and activities.

WEBSITE 5 Watch dinosaur videos, play quizzes and meet dinosaur hunters.

WEBSITE 6 An interactive virtual tour of a dinosaur exhibition.

WEBSITE 7 Meet Sue, the largest, most complete and best-preserved Tyrannosaurus rex fossil.

WEBSITE 8 Interactive dinosaur activities.

WEBSITE 9 Go on virtual dinosaur digs, see some amazing fossil discoveries and meet dinosaur hunters.

MUSEUM GUIDE

Many museums around the world have exhibits of skeletons, models of dinosaurs, fossils and other prehistoric exhibits. Here are some examples:

UK

The Natural History Museum, London;
University Museum of Natural History, Oxford;
The Sedgwick Museum, University of Cambridge;
Ulster Museum, Belfast;
The Royal Museum of Scotland, Edinburgh;
Museum of Isle of Wight Geology, Isle of Wight.

USA

American Museum of Natural History, New York;
Carnegie Museum of Natural History, Pittsburgh, PA;
Dinosaur National Monument, Vernal, UT;
Field Museum of Natural History, Chicago, IL;
Museum of Paleontology, Berkeley, University of California, CA;
Museum of the Rockies, Bozeman, MT;
National Museum of Natural History, Smithsonian Institution, Washington D.C.;
Peabody Museum of National History, Yale University, New Haven, CT.

CANADA

Canadian National Museum of Natural Sciences, Ottawa;
Royal Ontario Museum, Toronto;
The Royal Tyrell Museum of Paleontology, Alberta.

AUSTRALIA

Museum Victoria, Melbourne;
Australian Museum, Sydney;
Queensland Museum, Brisbane.

CONTINENTAL EUROPE

Belgium: Institut Royal des Sciences Naturelles de Belgique, Brussels;
France: Muséum National d'Histoire Naturelle, Paris;
Germany: Museum für Naturkunde, Berlin;
Senckenburg Museum, Frankfurt am Main.

INDEX

Where more than one page number is listed for a topic, the **bold** numbers show you where to find the main pages.

This edition first published in 2006 by
Usborne Publishing Ltd., Usborne House,
83-85 Saffron Hill, London EC1N 8RT,
England. www.usborne.com
Copyright © 2006, 2000, 1985, 1980
Usborne Publishing Ltd. The name Usborne
and the devices ♀ ☂ are Trade Marks of
Usborne Publishing Ltd.

UE. First published in America 2006.
Printed in Chennai, Tamil Nadu, India

Paw Prints

To

The Universe

A Puppy's Adventures and Journey

April Crawford

A "Memoir" Based Upon Actual Events

Title: **Paw Prints To *The Universe:***

A Puppy's Adventures and Journey: A "Memoir"

Based Upon Actual Events

Author: April Crawford

Publisher: Connecting Wave
2629 Foothill Blvd.
Unit # 353
La Crescenta, CA 91214
www.ConnectingWave.com

ISBN: 978-0-578-57285-7

For Author Information:
www.AprilCrawford.com

Other books via April Crawford:
www.AprilCrawfordBooks.com

Book Design: Allen Crawford

Contributing: Toni Sipka (a.k.a "Maha")

For Permissions: Publisher@ConnectingWave.com

Introduction

"I heard today that there is an invisible being that made everything. It is a huge presence that keeps track of all beings so that nothing bad happens to them. The mother licked my face in the yard behind the abandoned house. It felt so peaceful being lost underneath her. There was another besides myself that mother said was my brother. He tried to steal my milk from me when we ate from the teats of our mother. Her tongue would take the dirt from or ears and the soot from our eyes. There was nothing more blissful than her breath on our cheeks. Surely this was heaven. Surely I was here in this place to prosper and grow up with this brother of mine.

There were other animals in this place of repose. Some chatted with each other, some ever whispered amongst all the beings. The one who spoke of the Supreme Being claimed that we were all made from its vibration. That was such a big thought….. vibration. Certainly much bigger that I or even my brother. That's what my mother said he was anyways.

Introduction

It was too much to think about. Too big for sure. It was called the Universe. Another word way too big for puppy thoughts. That's what we are, puppies. If I try to find the vibration I can't. The mother says the universe will take care of us all. That feels good. Both my brother and I believe her. We both settle into the covered porch she found for us. Surely the Universe knows we are here. I ask earnestly the question so that I can relax.

Each day the warmth called the sun peeks through the cracks in the porch. Often we feel the warmth before we see the light. My brother's nose touches mine stealing my air with every breath. I do not mind. It makes me feel good to know he is that close.

The mother leaves early to find us food. She tells us to stay under that porch. We had hoped for time to play but she insisted we lay low to keep safe.

Not that we always did as we were asked. Many a day was spent under the tree waiting for the scent of the mother to fill the air. We disobeyed but felt the air upon our whiskers. Besides, we had made a few friends, at least we thought they were friends.

Ah! What did we know? It was all fun and games 'til the mother returned. Her tongue upon our ears told us she loved us. We would always bask in the light of her growl. She brought us morsels of food without asking. Her milk warm in our bellies. Being alive was working out well. The mother snuggled up beside us and we felt safe within her furry grasp.

Sometimes when I sleep I see others who try to talk to me. Who are they?

I know what humans are but do not know why they exist. A small male one threw stones at us once when we played in the grass. It surprised me for we had not been mean to him. The mother said they were all like that. Just plain mean. I recall watching the human walk away. He looked small like he was somewhat a puppy too. Maybe he just did not know any better. I wished that we could be friends. There was a memory of being held by a human. It was a female. I could see the blue eyes and they sparkled.

Introduction

My nose nestled at her neck felt wonderful. Would I see her again?

The mother scolded me for day dreaming.

"Puppies need to pay attention!" She growled.

So I paid attention.

I found out many things. There were and are a lot of creatures in this place. As I cuddled some more with my brother many of them came by to say hello. The mother seemed to know everyone. I wished so hard to know the why about everything. There were many tales told. Some just stories, while others made my heart pound.

One thing was for sure. There was this being that started everything. I wondered if it was a puppy like me. I wanted to see it for myself, but the mother said I was too young.

Introduction

"Why don't you talk to the Universe in your head? Humans write letters I heard, maybe you could do that!"

Big questions need answers. Why was I here? Why do bad things happen? (Like the time a cat got smacked by a metal being. I later was told it was a car, but that did not change the fact that the cat was left there on the street in a heap.)

So I have chosen to write to the Universe in my head. Maybe I would get some answers. Maybe I would see the face of the girl who loved me so much. Maybe just maybe I would discover my purpose under that porch of the human house. It was abandoned by humans but perfect for puppies waiting to grow up."

~ A Young Puppy

Introduction

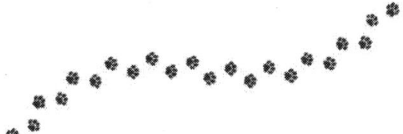

1

A Big Job For A New Puppy

Dear Universe,

I suppose you heard my request for the sky water to stop. After being so cold and wet it feels good o feel the body heat of my brother against me. The drips that hit us both on the head continue, but at least our fur is starting to dry out. I worry about the cough my brother seems to be doing. It can be very soft then exploding into a thunderstorm of hacking that is endless. Sometimes I lay on the top of him so that he will get warm and sleep. I stay awake during these times to be sure we are both safe. It's a big job for a puppy like me, but he is all I have these days.

We still stay under the shelter of the old porch. No one can see us. I keep hoping the mother will return to fetch us. Alas she has not. The drops of water roll down our heads into our dry mouths. It is of little comfort, but we still are here. What will happen to us I do not know. We have tasted many bugs as they scamper by. It is not enough to feel good, but it is better than nothing. I want to live! So does my brother, but he continues to sleep a lot. Maybe he is just tired of being hungry. There was a mouse that ran by..... I should have stopped it. I should have eaten him and so should have my brother.

What is to become of us?

Why am I here?

Maybe it was just to get wet and die??? That just seems wrong! Our mother did not even stay to love us? Why? If you are the wise Universe that has been told to all, then you should know. Right? You should know.

Please tell me how to live. Do we stay here? Will we ever be warm and dry?

Please tell me. My brother asks everyday and I have no answers.

2

Are You There?

Dear Universe,

Ok. So today is a better day. The light in the sky feels so good. There was a bird that fell down and we ate it after it died. It was the first time in a while that we both felt good. I guess food is important.

I decide to name my brother Blade. It's because he wants to smell every piece of plant life that he can. The blue jay told us that the soft stuff is called grass. It is made of little things called blades. Since Blade wants to sniff everyone I decided "Blade" was a good name for him.

I thought about a name for myself but was left speechless on the subject. Blade said I should name myself "Love" since I spend so much time loving him. It didn't seem right to decide upon a name. So for now I am just "Me".

We ventured out from our shelter into the light. A creature walked by that we were not familiar with. It stopped and stooped down to our faces. It spoke quietly while gesturing something towards up. It spilled upon the ground bouncing in all directions. It smelled funny but we certainly wanted to know what it was.

For a moment I was scared. What if the creature meant us harm? Both Blade and I were small. So far things had not gone very well.

Blade jumped ahead of me to start eating the nuts as they settled into the dirt. I yelled for him to stop! It might not be good for us. My heart was racing, my ears listening for direction but no one came to help us.

If you are the Universe and all knowing, why did you not save us? Why don't you find our mother? Okay the nuts were much needed food, but what if they had been poison? We are but babies left unprotected. Please send us some help.

Pawprints To The Universe

I feel better now. We both do. Food in the belly was welcome. Neither of us had been this satisfied since our mother's milk. Are you there?

3

It Was A Girl

Dear Universe,

So the creature turned out to be nice. Blade loved her.... yeah it was a girl. She scratched all the places that needed to be scratched. She spoke softly while letting us sniff her hand. My brother was and is a "sell out". He would follow her back to her space if I allowed it. I was adamant that we wait 'til our mother returned. He thought the creature was nice. We had learned from a tomcat that she was a human. She often came to feed those like ourselves, albeit it was rumored that some disappeared never to return.

True to my gut feelings I stayed aloof from her. What if she kidnapped us? Then we would surely never see our mother again. Blade did not believe in the mother anymore. He was also convinced that there is no invisible energy called the Universe. Our

Pawprints To The Universe

best hope was that the girl would still bring us food while rubbing our ears. All we wanted was food and shelter. Water had not fell from the sky for a while. He thought it was just luck. I like to think you heard my pleas and made it stop. It's so good to be warm and fed.

4

Blade Is Scared

Dear Universe,

Where did the mother go? We wait with vigilance under the porch for many days. I know you are in touch with all things living. Tell her to come home. Blade is scared. I am too but I must put on a brave face to my brother. He is still too small. Why does he not get bigger as I have? We eat the same things. The mother's milk no longer fills us. I worry that Blade will not wake up each morning. If you are truly watching out for us, then send someone to help us. Better yet send the mother to us. I fear something bad has befallen her.

5

The Mother

Dear Universe,

The mother has not returned. Both Blade and I fear the worst. Something bad has befallen her. Can you see where she is? Being in your spot must be easy for you to locate her. I know she would not leave us here to die. My belly is empty. It growls while Blade whimpers for food. I was told you are all powerful. Why can you not send someone to help us?

6

Searching For Food

Dear Universe,

I was thinking today of how small I am in the big picture. In fact it's been a new thing to even consider that there are things too large to understand. I guess I wonder why I am even here. What reason is there for me to live? It feels like I am stuck in the wrong place at the wrong time. Is that true?

My head aches sometimes when there is no food. The grass by the door tastes pretty good but doesn't make my belly feel full. I remember someone left some human food near where my brother and I were. It smelled funny but we at it all up. So fast. We both felt a little woozy afterward but at least the grinding emptiness stopped for a while. And no. I do not like the red stuff..... a cat told me it was called ketchup.

Pawprints To The Universe

I see many humans but they do not see me, of this I am sure. So backing up to my first question..... Why? Why am I here? So hungry. So cold. Feeling like my brother needs more from me than I can give? This place is so scary. Shouldn't it be better? Shouldn't you dear Universe tell them I am here? My brother says I am too arrogant, that I should eat what I can while forgetting about these lofty ideas about reason and purpose. He may be right since nothing has gone well since our mother disappeared. I still feel the warmth of her belly as she cradled us in her love. It seems like so very long ago. Maybe she will come back someday. Maybe.

Maybe not.

I know I should not worry, but dear Universe the ache in my belly tells me it most likely will not, even if I wish it so. Why do wishes not come true? It seems a simple question so why not a straight answer?

The tail wags without my awareness every time the idea of food enters my mind. We (brother and I) walk quietly to the place of food the humans go to. The last time we were here we found the bag I spoke of earlier. There is great hope a bag will befall us soon as the humans toss extra food into cylinder objects. It is well known that they often miss, spilling the wonderful contents into the ground. We gladly oblige with clean up duty. Again, I always sniff out the ketchup. Blade gobbles it up. We make a good team together.

7

Decision Made

Dear Universe,

Today a human came into the yard. We could see the feet move closer from our porch. Blade began to cry again as a face peered into our home.

"Come out little puppy. I won't hurt you!"

I was reluctant but of course my brother stuck his snout as far out as he could. Before I could cry out, the human snatched him up. My heart began to beat faster as I yelled at the human to put him down. Blade the traitor licked the face of the intruder and I just knew we were doomed. Yelling as loud as I could, hoping to scare the human into dropping my trusting brother.

It did not work.

"Oh my god! There is another puppy!"

The eyes of the intruder seemed kind. The mother had always said humans were just plain mean. Is that true?

I need guidance now. The hands reach towards me as I recoil as far back as possible.

"Come out little buddy. Come get with your brother. I won't hurt you."

There was a choice to be made. Either I snapped at this human or I succumbed to the reaching hands.

What do I do Universe?

While waiting for our answer, my empty stomach decided. The human had food. Decision made.

8

Going Somewhere Else

Dear Universe,

Are humans trustworthy? I can't tell. The female who fed us did so with apparent strings attached. While we filled our bellies she somehow put a loop around our necks. Why? I was startled at first so I behaved poorly. Blade was so busy eating he did not notice.

I was afraid. Why would she suddenly break the trust she established? Before we knew it we were put into boxes with holes. I yelled as loud as I could hoping the mother would reappear to rescue us. It was not to be.

The cat who was our friend perched on the fence watching it all unfold.

"Help us", I screamed. "If the mother comes back tell her what happened."

"Sure, sure I will", he replied.

With an abrupt swing the box we were trapped in left the porch. The only home we ever knew. Where was she taking us? Surely the all powerful Universe knows something.

Blade whimpered as he stuck his snout under my leg. At least we are together.

If you are listening Universe, we need help.

The box landed in another box that moved miraculously on its own. We were behind the female. A roar of noise left us both scared and confused.

"Don't worry puppies! It's gonna be okay. I am taking you to a safer place."

I squinted one of my eyes. I could see the light in the sky. Lots of things whooshed by us. We were obviously going somewhere else. Blade cried beside

Pawprints To The Universe

me. Please dear Universe. Keep me brave for both
of us.

9

What Is This Place?

Dear Universe,

Okay. So we are both still alive. The human left us in this strange place. It appears that others are here as well. We can hear the crying of many who feel they have been abandoned. Are we to join them? There was some food and water brought to our place. There are no warm spots except for each other. What is this place?

I want to thank the Universe for keeping us safe so far. There are no lights in the sky. It's the first time I have not felt wind on my face.

I miss the lights in the sky. At least it is not wet. Blade and I curled up together as close as we could. There was darkness with weird sounds throughout the sleep time. We will see what the new day brings. Please dear Universe protect us.

10

Humans Talk A Lot But...

Dear Universe,

I heard you speak to me. Thank you for the encouragement. This human place is a fearful one. The crying of the others sings continuously. No one comes to comfort those who are scared. I cannot be afraid as my brother needs me to be strong. When they come to bring food he hides behind me. I stare straight into their eyes as the mother taught me. They speak not to me, but they are not mean. There is a blank look in their eyes. It is something I have not seen before. Are they really human? Or are they aliens like the Pit Bull in the next cubicle claims?

I wish I could be next to you dear Universe so that I could hear your better. It's really tough to be brave. All I really want is the mother. Somehow though I know she is not coming back.

Pawprints To The Universe

The cough of Blade worsens but he does eat his food. I will wrap myself around him more this evening. I plan on willing him better. I want to dream of the girl again too. She has been in my head a few more times. Thank you dear Universe for listening. I have really no one to guide me but you. Being in this place is hard. No one listens. Humans talk a lot but need help with the hearing. It would be different I think if they listened.

11

Humans Are Strange

Dear Universe,

It is noisy all the time here. Mostly there are other dogs crying. Why do they cry? Are they missing the mother too?

The whispers told of stories about the sadness and hardship. It feels strange to be here. Both Blade and I wish to be back under the porch. If the mother does come back, how will she find us? I don't believe the cat will tell her. Blade believes she will. At least there is food. Thank you dear Universe for that. Now if only we can see the sky again it might be ok.

Humans are strange. Some come to this place just looking into our spaces. What are they looking for? Blade nestles close beside me while we wait, but for what? Please send me some answers. All I

Pawprints To The Universe

want is for us both to be safe. Blade threw up his food today. The human was not happy. I postured in front of Blade to be sure he would not get into trouble. The human cleaned it up but was mean. The mother always said they were just plain mean. I believe she was right.

12

The Female With Blue Eyes

Dear Universe,

We are still here in this place. The cries from some of the others keep us awake at night. The Pit Bull next to us has disappeared. He was there on moment, not the next. It is rumored he was killed but I choose to believe he was set free. Others feel that maybe someone came to take him home. I like that idea. It makes me thing about the female with blue eyes. I see her in my head all the time. Maybe she will show up and take Blade and I home. Do you think it could happen Dear Universe?

Blade doesn't think so.

Sometimes he cries for the mother. I think about her too. If she came back and found us gone was she sad? Would she come looking for us?

Pawprints To The Universe

The lights in the place go dark and I am with just my memories and the beating heart of my brother Blade. Please dear Universe take care of us. Help me to find the female who loves us. It feels like I need to find her. Please help us.

13

The Humans Came With
A Weird Thing

Dear Universe,

Remind me why I came to such a desolate weird place. At least under the porch I could feel the ground. It had life to it. This place is cold and unforgiving.   The hard stone does not provide comfort. It hurts my feet if I stand too long. Blade never complains but he stumbles a lot when he gets up. He cries in pain when he lays down too fast. Is this the best I can do? Why is it so hard?

The humans come and go in the midst of chaos caused by so many of us displaced. I wish the mother would come get us.

Oh! And the humans came with a weird thing that put symbols on Blade and I. It hurt a little, well,

Pawprints To The Universe

actually a lot. They said it was so they would know who we were. Know who we are? I know who I am. You, the Universe knows who we are. The symbols look odd. I tried to lick them off but to no avail.

The Universe needs to step in and do something. I want my home back. I want to be under the porch with the mother. I have heard you can do anything! At least that's what I heard. Please do something!

14

The Human With Blue Eyes

Dear Universe,

There are many stories that circulate in this place. I have heard many through the thick stone walls. Some say we were brought here to die. That there are just too many of us and some just need to go. If it weren't for Blade I would be so cold. The floor is also made of stone. It echoes the cries of the others that were also brought here.

I found out we are known as dogs. Yep, that's what we are called. Another Pit Bull (which is a kind of dog) told me that there was a chance that a human would come to take us to their home. That worries me because as far as I know humans are mean. Most do not like dogs, so why wold one of them take us home?

Pawprints To The Universe

The only human I know who is kind is the one who comes to see me in my dreams. Did you send her to me dear Universe? Is she real?

I can see her eyes and they are blue. Most of the time I do not see color but in the dream I see it very well.

15

A Puppy Can Only Hope

Dear Universe,

Today there were many humans walking by our space. Some of them were little so I think they are like me. I am a puppy still and so is Blade. I could hear laughter along with dog barks. It sounded fun. I poked my snout as far as I could into the bars. Blade kept sleeping, not at all interested in what was going on. Sometimes I worry about him. He just seems to lay there without much energy. I ask him if he is ok but he always answers, "Yes, I am ok". After which he rolls over and goes back to sleep.

I, on the other hand always have much going on inside. There is still hope the mother will return, but so far nothing.

A few humans looked in the space today and asked "are these two ready?" Ready for what? This is our home now. We are waiting to go back to our under porch home. Somehow. Some day. We will get back to our home. In the meantime we are here.

What do you see for us dear Universe? Are we going to get to go home? It looks bleak but I am always full of hope.

The attendant opens the door to give us water and food. At least that has been good. Our bellies full, we both cuddle up to sleep. That can be hard if others cry out in the night.

I close my eyes tightly so I can see her face. She comforts me most nights. Maybe she will show up here.

A puppy can only hope.

16

When We Are Bigger

Dear Universe,

Since I have been here in this place I have seen more humans then I ever have before. No one told me that there were so many of them. From my spot with Blade, millions of them walk by every day. Some look in with smiles, but many of them scowl at us with squinty eyes. Blade doesn't really notice cause he sleeps so much. Since I am still a puppy I have a lot of extra energy. Sometimes I get all jittery inside. It's like if I don't run real fast I will just explode. Blade usually laughs about my jitters. He says that he has never felt them. So who is having truer experience? Me or him? I wish he would bounce around with me but he says he is too tired. I worry about him sometimes. At least we are dry with food. It tastes yucky, but sometimes I am so hungry I don't care. Blade lets me have what he doesn't eat.

Pawprints To The Universe

My paws are getting bigger! I wonder if that means I will get bigger. Does size make a difference in the world? I think if I were bigger I could protect my brother and me. After all someday when we are grown we can go back to the porch to live. By then we will both be big enough to survive on our own. If the mother comes bck we can take care of her too.

17

The Humans Are Coming Closer

Dear Universe,

The more I observe these humans the more surprised I get. Each day a male one comes by with food and water. He looks sad all the time. He throws the food into our space so hard the little pieces bounce off the wall behind us. Blade thinks he is just stupid. I think he has thoughts in his head that that he can't figure out. I try to say hi to him but he never really looks at me. It's like he is somewhere else. Are all of them like this? This place is strange. I wonder if we will ever get out of here. I want to see the little lights in the sky again. I don't miss getting wet though. Sometimes I hear it hitting the walls outside. I wonder if there are other puppies getting all wet. Maybe someone will rescue them like we were.

I have lots of time to think in this place. No one seems to care enough to come talk to us. The dog across the hallway says we ae invisible to them. The only time we are seen is when someone comes to take one of us home with them.

I wonder what that would be like? Of course they would have to take Blade too. We are brothers and he depends on me.

I hear footsteps coming down the corridor. There must be three or four of them. What would they want right now? A small bug crawls slowly down the wall. It seems intently making a path to a crack under the door. Maybe he could escape that way. Putting my snout near the door crack I could just about see those making footsteps down the hall. It was two men and a girl. It seems they are looking in each of the spaces for something.

Wake up Blade! His sleepy eyes barely opened.

"What?" he mumbled.

"Humans are coming close", I whispered. They will be here soon. I glanced down at the bug as it slid through the door crack. Lucky critter! I realized how I longed to be able to do that….. just slip under the door.

18

What Does That Mean?

Dear Universe,

The woman leaned towards me as she squealed in delight. "Oh! Isn't he cute?" Searching her face looking for confirmation that this was my dream girl come to life. Her face was close to mine as I realized that there was not any way that this was she. The eyes did not glisten in the light. There was a vacant look that made her appear a bit scary. What was she doing here?

Here voice rang through the corridor announcing her intention to adopt me. Adopt me? What does that mean? I have heard you dear Universe many times, but this female was not within any of our conversations. I don't know her. Never did. Hopefully never will.

Glancing at Blade he is again asleep. I worry that his breathing isn't right. Sometimes I listen to him while we are both supposed to be sleeping. The door of our space opens and the female reaches in to grab me. Uhm no. I do not want to leave the space. Realizing that I would need to comply or outright bite her. I chose to be compliant.

Blade opened one eye and started to bark a little.

"Do you want them both?" a voice asked.

"No. Just him" was the reply.

Panic set into me as I realized I was him.

19

Adoption

Dear Universe,

Today was the worst day ever. A female human adopted me! My last glimpse of Blade ws over her shoulder as we marched out of sanctuary. I kept barking long after his little head was out of view. Please take care of him! He is not well. He's bit weaker than I and he needs someone to take care of him. It's just too much this separation. It might be better if she could understand me. I would tell her to go back and get him.

Maybe I can escape. When she is not looking. There does not seem to be too much thinking going on inside her head. At first I thought she just might be the one I have dreamed about. Alas that was not so.

Pawprints To The Universe

Before we left I was given some medicine with a needle. It hurt so bad but not as much as my heart leaving Blade behind.

I should have been excited.

I should have been relieved.

They told me that I was going to a new home! That was all great but without my brother my empty heart was all I had.

She put me in a car. I had seen them before but never had been inside one. The odd smell was like no other. Trust me. Under the porch there had been a lot of odd smells. This one was different. It was the scent of a human. Hers was bigger because she blew smoke out of her mouth. Maybe she would burn up and I could go back to my brother. I watched her stare out of the window. She did not look at me. Why did she adopt me if she wasn't going to say hi to me? Weird.

20

In The House

Dear Universe,

Now I know that this is definitely not the female human of my dreams. This one gets angry….. a lot. The house again smelled weird. There was continuous smoke out of her mouth. She scratched my ears a few times then fell asleep. I sat watching her breathe wondering how it was I came to be here. If I had a life plan, it certainly had gone awry.

My stomach felt hungry. Wondering if she planned on feeding me. Maybe there was water somewhere. Never had I been in a human home before. Yes, there was the porch but it was outside of the house it was attached to.

Watching the human I slid stealthily off the chair. Maybe I should just look for food myself. No time like the present to see what was available.

My toenails clicked rhythmically on the ground. It did not lend itself to sneaking around. She could wake up any second.

A deep sigh came from her while I was looking in a room the looked like it may have food. After a deep investigation I found nothing but a lump of something. There was no time to be picky. Swallowing it quickly it did calm my growling belly.

No water in sight.

"Hey Puppy".

Oh no. It was her. Should I answer? Should I hide. No time to consider, I walked back to where she had been sleeping.

She was sitting up on her elbows smiling at me. There was a wrinkle in her forehead that twitched a lot. I was pretty sure that she was crazy, rather like the alley cat near the porch. He would beat anyone up. Even if they had not done anything. Then he would come back around hoping you would share

your food. The mother said he just had that look…..
crazy.

So it was with this female. Not wanting to cross
her, I approached her space timidly.

"Come on sweetie. Come on! Oh you're just too
cute!

She spoke with authority so I moved closer. May
be she would be nice to me? After all she found me
and brought me here. Maybe she would give me
food, My throat was so dry, a little water would feel
good right about now.

Slowly, slowly, slowly, I moved towards her
extended hand. Time to make friends I supposed.
My growling belly was so hungry. I bet she would
know if there was really food in the other room. Her
fingertips brushed my snout. It felt good. Scooting
a little closer her face was suddenly so close to mine.
Her breath smelled funny.

21

Growling Real Soft

Dear Universe,

Ok. I am in the clutches of a crazy human? How did this happen? I thought it would go better than this!

She's happy. She's sad. She's crazy!

When she patted my head she smiled then she slapped my snout because I did not respond correctly? She calls me her "little puppy" in a funny voice, then gets mad for no reason at all. I need help figuring this out dear Universe. Just because I am a puppy doesn't mean I am stupid. Don't slap me for no reason!

I moved directly away as quickly as I could. My belly now screaming, my mouth parched for a drop of water. Do you think she will give me some? What do I do?

I tried growling real soft but not too close to where she lay. She had to know I would need food. This whole story of how being adopted would provide food and a family somehow now looks like a lie. The mother would never have left me without food. Well except for the last time that she didn't come back.

Sigh.

I guess I will wait on the other side of this place to see what happens. At least in the space with Blade we got food and water.

Please check on him dear Universe. Hoepfully he is still there. He's not strong like me. If he gets someone like this one he will not survive.

22

I Decide To Investigate

Dear Universe,

It is becoming apparent that this female human is just plain mean. Exactly what the mother used to say. She fell back asleep so I decided to investigate. There had to be food somewhere. My belly hurt so it was not a choice, it was a must have.

The floor was slick, especially in a couple of the rooms. There was a huge white bowl of water that looked like it had a lid. Up on my tip toes I could see water inside. There was a bunch of it, which was very exciting. I couldn't quite get my snout down to it. Being resourceful, the back of the bowl looked like I could get up on it. My throat so dry was eager for a few gulps of water. Jumping on my back legs it was easy to get up on it. The water was so close I could almost feel it in my throat already. Just a few more inches and then it was disaster.

My paws slipped and I fell head first into the bowl.   Thrashing around trying to find balance seemed endless.   What if I died?   What if I got stuck? A lot of pictures flashed through my head. It was the final picture of the female human coming through the door that scared me the most.

"What are you doing?   You little wretch.   The toilet? Really? Bad dog. Bad dog!

23

Water

Dear Universe,

I now am in full agreement with the mother. Humans are just plain mean.

This female who adopted me is so hateful. Firstly, she talks to me like I am stupid. Just because I can't make the noise like she does, does not mean I am a dumb dog. Nor am I a bad dog. I was a thirsty dog. No one gave me water. So I did the best I could. Under the porch there was a leak in a pipe that gave water to the mother, me, and Blade. I ws given a bowl of water in the shelter space. So how was I supposed to find water in a strange place. I barked at the female many times, but she did not wake up.

Sheesh!

Pawprints To The Universe

I just needed some water!

The female yelled at me for a long time. She jerked the collar she put on me real hard. For a minute I thought I would spit up.

Once she stopped yelling, she left me by myself. That was fine with me, but..... I was still hungry. I decided it was worth the risk to complain a little, so I waited till she looked like she might be awake..... then I started to growl softly. Maybe she would feed me.

One can only hope.

24

Good and Bad, In That Order

Dear Universe,

She finally put some food on the floor. It looked funny, but by this time I was so hungry I did not care. It was different than the shelter space. It did not have a lot of flavor but it did do the trick. My belly stopped hurting. The female human sat down again looking into an odd box of people (like humans) talking. I didn't understand what it was but she looked down at me. In a split second she invited me to come be with her. No one ever asked me to be with them before, especially a human. Excited, I jumped up next to her. It was warm and cozy. Settled next to her I had a moment of great comfort. Maybe this would not be so bad after all. I let my guard down and snuggled in.

Sleep in a soft bed was something I had never experienced. So warm. So soft. The voices in the box rambled on as I fell asleep. The female human touched my ears. It was an incredible feeling! Perhaps I had been wrong! Perhaps this was the human I had dreamed of! Maybe it was all going to be good.

She stopped scratching my ears as she too fell asleep. All in all, this turned out to be a pretty good day. I wondered how Blade was. Maybe I could talk this human into going back to get him. We could all be a happy family. Me, Blade, and the female human. It could be so good!

My eyes closed and I was asleep.

If I could just hold onto this moment all would be well. And it was..... until I felt my pee wanting to be released. In the shelter space Blade and I just peed. Under the porch we peed out on the grass as to not soil our home. The mother insisted that we do so.

Here.

Here, what do I do?

I tried to keep it inside. I really did.

I growled a little to ask the human what she wanted me to do.

She was fast asleep. There was no way to ask her what she wanted me to do. So, I did the only thing I could do. I jumped down on the floor and peed on the floor. The was no other choice that I knew of.

I jumped back on the couch and waited for her to wake up. That did not happen until the sun had risen. By then the pee scent was strong and I needed to do it again. The only other choice I could think of was to pee in this makeshift human bed. Somehow that did not seem to be a good choice.

I had just finished my second pee when her eyes opened.

"Oh my god! What are you doing you little brat! Are you peeing on the floor?"

She jumped up and chased me around the room screaming the whole time.

"Bad dog!"

"Bad dog."

I was so scared. It seemed she meant me great harm. No way was she going to catch me! The mother was right all along. Humans a just plain mean.

25

So...

Dear Universe,

So she finally did catch me. She slapped my behind for peeing on the floor.

"Why didn't you go outside? She screamed. Her breathing was funny like she was out of breath. She was wiping up the mess I made, sounding just terrible.

My dear Universe, could you let her know that if she wants me to go outside she needs to open the door and let me outside? I held it as long as I could because I really do want to be a good boy. This whole adoption isn't going well. Can I get sent back to the shelter space? At least there was not yelling there. Blade might also still there..... maybe.

Pawprints To The Universe

She finally got quiet, but I continued hiding under the table. The food was scattered on the floor half out of the bag. If one were to sneak over there, they might get to eat some of it.

I waited until I was sure she was asleep. A light form the other room not yet explored guided me to the morsels. Tried to chew quietly, hoping to get to eat most of it before discovery. The last piece was in my mouth when she suddenly picked me up.

"Come here puppy. Come sleep with me!"

Sleep with her? Do I have to?

Supposedly it was required. The blanket covered me up and for a moment I remembered the mother tyring to keep my brother and I warm. The thought of those times felt good. My eyes closed as the warmth and softness took effect.

It was apparent the female human was crazy. Kind of like the rough tomcat that used to scare Blade and myself. You never knew what to expect from him. I guess she was like that too.

Pawprints To The Universe

So dear Universe, if you can help me escape from this madness I will love you forever. If there is a point to all this I sure have missed it. Keep me safe tonight. Oh, and keep Blade safe too. I want to see him again sometime.

26

With All Four Paws!

Dear Universe,

Things are getting much worse. This morning she still slept while I was wide awake. Water was needed as my throat was scratchy from being thirsty. The food from last night started to churn until I knew I needed to poop and soon.

Peeking over her I could see outside. Pooping there would be no problem. Thing was, I had to get there first. Maybe I should wake her up? Or I could just sneak out. Problem was how to get out.

I felt a cramp that signaled that I needed to figure out soon. It was easy to jump over her. Trotting into the room with the huge white bowl, I felt a sudden panic realizing that it was already too late to get outside. She was sure to be mad about this.

Could I hide it? No.

Could I get it out of here? No.

In the process I managed to step in it with all four paws. Oh no! Now it was everywhere.

"Puppy?"

"Where are you?"

Oh no. She was awake.

I had to acknowledge her call. Risking discovery, I peeked into where she lay.

She was going to be mad.

27

Maybe She Will Remember

Dear Universe,

The mother used to tell us that everything has a cost. At the time I did not know what she meant. She loved me and fed me. In the day when it was safe we would sit in the sun. Those times are still in my heart. When I get yelled at those thoughts help me live through it.

This human female was very mad. She slapped my snout, then rubbed it into the poop on the floor. She scared me so much. I did not know what else to do. It was coming out no matter what. Why was she so mean? There was no place else to do it!

Someone told me once that you were God. That seems so small of a word for such a huge presence. The mother talked of you often. She said that everything has its place and that you, the Universe, helped those like us. If you could, please help me. This place is not filled with the love I hoped for. The female is still mad about the accident. I tried to explain but she left me by myself for a whole night. Not knowing if she would ever return, I turned to finding that food bag again.

Yes.

It was right where she left it. Closed, but with a few bites I had it open. The ache in my belly stopped within the first few bites. There was no water, but the big white bowl in the small room still had some in it.

The darkness was scary all by myself, but the chair was comfortable. Circling around, I gathered in the energy as the mother had taught me. Too bad Blade was not here to cuddle. His warm belly would have comforted me in my loneliness. Would the female return? I was conflicted about it. Part of me wanted to never see her again. The other part hoped for her return.

Why is it dear Universe that I cannot find my true partner.? Why is there such a mystery around it?

All I want is to be home. Cuddles with Blade with the hand of the human who is my true friend. I fear that I will never find her. My eyes are heavy, the blanket feels so soft against my skin.

I promised myself that I will try harder to please her. Maybe she will remember that I am a living being. Food and water are needed. The ability to eliminate what I eat is very important. I can't control what is just a natural process. She gets so mad when I can't.

Drifting off I hear a hum of energy in another room. It's almost like a lullaby. The mother used to lick our ears to soothe us. Wishing she was here right now.

28

A Name

Dear Universe,

She came home with another human. I think it's a male. There is laughing and stumbling about. Hidden behind the couch I hope she forgets I am here.

"Oh! Where is my puppy?" she said a little too loudly.

"Where are you little boy?"

She was acting strange! My only hope was to sit very still. Maybe they would forget I was here. Maybe not.

"Puppy!!!"

Scooped up into her arms there was a feeling she would drop me. Whoa!!! She almost did.

"Here's my new puppy! Isn't he cute?" she mumbled. "Puppy, meet your new Dad!"

With that she literally threw me at the male who somehow caught me.

"What's his name?" he asked.

"He doesn't have one", she replied.

"Hey I could use another beer. Do you have a Guinness?"

"Um. Maybe. Let me go look."

The male began scratching my head. I felt a little safer with him. So far, he had not dropped me. I guess that was good.

"Look! I have a Guinness!" she said upon her return.

"Hey! Let's call the pup Guinness?"

Pawprints To The Universe

"After the beer?"

"No, after my Irish heritage. I think it fits him."

"What do you think Guinness?"

What did I think?

I thought both of them were crazy. Wanting to be loved and accepted I would have responded to anything. Guinness? OK, that had a nice ring to it.

Left suddenly to my own devices I heard them mating. The mother said this was the way of things. Hopefully they would quiet soon. The good news was that I had a name. Never had that before. Maybe things were looking up.

29

A Bit Crazy

Dear Universe,

Boy, having a name isn't all it's cracked up to be. I thought everyone would just call me Guinness with great love and affection. It meant I was no longer just a stray. I had a home and I was Guinness.

It just wasn't the way I thought it would be. First of all the female was a bit crazy. She drank some sort of potion from a bottle and coughed….. a lot. The guy was nicer. He always remembered to take me out to pee. Most of the time he also thought to put food and water down. She hardly ever did.

Dear Universe, maybe you can help me understand what is wrong with her. It occurred to me that she just doesn't like dogs. Or maybe she is just plain mean like the mother used to say. Regardless, please help me figure it out. I'd still like to go back and get Blade. It would be nice to have a family here.

"Guinness NO!"

"Guinness GET DOWN!"

"Guinness, DID YOU MAKE THIS MESS?"

"GUINNESS! DID YOU JUST PEE ON THE FLOOR?

"GUINNESS, YOU ARE A BAD DOG".

It went on almost every day. I learned to make myself invisible like you suggested. My snout hurt from her last slap. Is this how it's going to always be?

At least the guy was nicer. Hopefully he would stick around for a while. He would pat my head while scratching my back. I never dreamed how good that would feel.

Thanks Universe for sticking with me. I don't know what I'd do without you.

30

It Comes When It Comes

Dear Universe,

The guy is now in charge of taking me outside to pee. The female says she is fed up with me and my antics. So the guy said he would make sure I was a good boy. He woke up before the sun every day. He was always in a hurry to go somewhere. My neck is sore from him jerking the leash. Sorry, but it won't make me pee any faster. It comes when it comes. You would think he would know that.

It still amazes me that these two are together. I have watched how they posture with each other and it's not good. They say they love each other and that they love me. Love me? Is this what humans call love? It's so confusing! It isn't possible that this is what love is. The mother feeding me while keeping me warm is more like love than this.

Pawprints To The Universe

The days come and go. Focused purely upon getting food while attempting to hold my pee is an exhausting experience. Tippy toe, while being as cute as possible has become the goal. If I can make it a few days without reproach there is great happiness.

I wonder how Blade is….. Did someone bring him to a home too? I guess I will never know. Please take care of him dear Universe. He's all that I have in this crazy world.

31

My Chance

Dear Universe,

Things have changed. Whatever a wedding is, I suppose it's happening. For some stupid reason it was decided there would be a bath for me. A bath? You mean with water? Why?

The question was not answered. The female handed me to another female demanding that she do the deed. It was like they were going to punish me. I had been very good, which wasn't easy in this crazy place.

Today there was a lot of people around. Everyone was laughing and talking. Hoping to be invisible a pair of hands lifted me into the air. Oh great, it was her in a funny white suit of some sort.

"Oh Guinness! Mama is going to get married today!"

"Give me a kiss you little boy."

I gave her a quick lick of the tongue just to shut her up. With any luck she would set me down and forget all about me.

I was right. In a few moments she was off laughing and giggling with someone new. As I waded through the people I noticed that the front door was wide open. Looking around to see who was looking, I move slowly towards it. You must have been guiding me dear Universe. This was my chance. Escape within my grasp!

There were a lot of people outside but I was feeling confident of success. I could find Blade! I could rescue us both! We could travel to another reality where there was plenty of food and warm blankets. Freedom within my eyesight. It was time to plunge headfirst into that void of freedom.

Here I go.

Here I go.

Almost there.

The breeze blew my fur back making me feel like super puppy. Nothing was to be held from me. I could see other houses while running as fast as I could.

Almost there….. almost there…..

"Hey Guinness! Someone catch the dog! Oh my God! Before he gets hurt….. grab him!"

The words pierced my heart. The prison break about to be foiled. I closed my eyes while making a last dash effort.

"Hey little Guy! What'cha doin'?" Lookin' up at a female who I did not know. Did you send her dear Universe?

It sure seemed like it. Her hands held me close as the air escaped me. Panting vigorously I felt a calmness despite all the hysteria in my capture.

Her face was warm. Her eyes sparkled with amusement. By some miracle she wasn't mad. That much ws a relief. She might have turned me into the crazy one for punishment, but she didn't. Instead she took me back into the house. Was she the one I was looking for?

32

Maha

Dear Universe,

She made me some food, which I ate vigorously. The mean one forgot to feed me this morning as usual. Something about her wedding day and how important that was. Actually I was used to being forgotten. The only attention I got was when something bad happened. The blame was always on me.

In my escape plan there would have been a reunion with my brother Blade. By now he must be worried sick. The mean one thinks I forgot about him, but no, that is not the case. It seems that humans simply don't understand how much we know and remember. If you're mean then you really don't get it. I hope Blade is doing okay. Maybe someone will understand and bring him here. Do you, the Universe, think that can happen? Tell me some good news, I need some.

The nice female talked to me while I ate. Seems she's not happy with the mean one. No surprises there. Gosh, she even stoked my back while I was eating. This is new.

All the people stood outside while the mean one and her man got married….. whatever that is. In the arms of the nice one I learned she was known as "Maha". That was a weird name for a human, but I was beginning to realize she was different.

Gazing into her eyes I realized she was truly a good human. Her embrace made me feel safe and secure. The last time I felt this way was with the mother. Did you send her to me dear Universe? I think you did.

33

Good For Me!

Dear Universe,

Whatever happened that day with the man and the mean one, it was good for me. Maha my new friend took me with her. The house grew smaller and smaller as I looked out the back window. That made me happy. It was said the mean one was now married and gone away with her new husband. The car noises lulled me asleep next to Maha. Her hand rested on my back, while every once in awhile scratching my ears. She said they were the biggest cutest ones she had ever seen. Imagine that. Me. Cute and adored by a remarkable human female. I had hoped she was the one, but I remembered that you said I would know right away. There was a hesitation in my heart when I thought about it, which made me quite unsure.

Pawprints To The Universe

I have decided to think about it tomorrow. Right now I was on my way to Maha's house. She said she had two puppies already. I wonder if one of them is Blade? Wouldn't that be a big surprise.

Life now seems worth living.

You were right dear Universe, things do get better. I have to learn to trust you more on that.

34

Thank You For Sending Me Here

Dear Universe,

I think I have arrived in heaven. There are two new dogs living here. Maha brought me in and it's so great! There's food, walks down to the rocks, and snuggle time. The last one I was not sure about. It seems everyone jumps in the bed to sleep. Everyone already had their spots so it was kind of difficult to squeeze in. So warm that it reminded me of the mother and Blade. I tried to ask Maha if she knew where they were. She does not understand reading my thoughts and I can't say her words with my snout. We do though connect with our hearts.

The two dogs are Tory and Shannon. They are all much bigger than me but that doesn't make them smarter. Tory is like the patriarch of the family. He loves his Maha a lot. He talks to her with thoughts, so it's hard to understand why she can't understand mine. Shannon is quiet. She is nice to me but she gets a little sick sometimes. All in all I am grateful dear Universe to be rid of the mean one. Thank you for sending me here. With any luck I will never see the mean one again.

35

Stay Here Guinness

Dear Universe,

I know you told me that sometimes bad things happen but in the end everything has a reason. I struggle as to what end this will come to. Most of the time I stay at the house of Maha. She is a good human. She loves me like her own. I get fed when they do and she takes me on walks.

The mean one sleeps a lot. At night she goes to some unknown place, often not returning until the first light of day. Actually that works great for me. In those times I often stay with Maha and I get to sleep in the bed with Shannon and Tory. Of course Maha is there too. It's cozy. There is no place I'd rather be. If it were this way for the rest of my life, it would be okay.

Only when the mean one wants to pretend she has a dog does it go poorly.

She decides to take me shopping but leaves me in the car.

She decides to get food for herself but forgets to get me some.

Sometimes she takes me outside to pee but gets mad if I don't do it fast enough. Sometimes I just can't help it.

If she drags me back inside too soon and I end up peeing on the floor, I am a bad dog. Why would I be in this woman's possession? You said that everything that should, matches up when in a body. Why then is she around me? What did I do wrong and what can I do to be free of her?

It's dark and cold outside. All I want to do is snuggle up with everyone. The mean one picks me up declaring that I am going to spend the evening with her. My heart sank as I looked desperately at Maha, hoping for a reprieve.

Maha tried to talk her out of it to no avail. The leather seat was cold and slippery. It made it even colder. The car started and we were off. Oh no! This could not have a good ending.

We drove for a long time before the mean one stoped the car.

"You stay here Guinness. I am going to have some fun!"

By this time I was too sleepy to care. The heater had warmed me up. Curled into a little ball, sleep had come quickly. The slam of the car door woke me up but all I could see was the back of her head as she went inside the building.

There were stars twinkling above making me wonder if you were watching over me. The mother always said that you never left. All I had to do was talk to you and you would listen. I hope so. Are you?

36

Welcomed Back

Dear Universe,

The night was long, the car became frigid while the stars twinkled down upon me. Since I was all curled up I managed to at least keep my belly and paws warm. The need to pee was very vivid, but if I peed in the car there would be no forgiveness for me.

The sun was beginning to peek out over the horizon. My belly hurt from holding the pee. Hope that she would return soon fueled my thoughts. I remember the mother telling me that if I thought about something long enough I could make it happen. So in the conflict of hoping she would never return, I thought about her opening the door. As the sun began to shine she showed up. She thought I was excited to see her but it was more my bladder than me. Bounding out of the car I peed for what seemed like forever. She pulled my leash several times wanting me to hurry up. This is what you get mean woman when you leave me alone all night in a car!

Before I knew it we were on our way home. That being Maha's house. The doors were locked but her puppies greeted us with enthusiasm..... Tory the patriarch giving me a good sniff to determine what I had be up to. I told him about spending the night in the car by myself. He was livid at the mean woman. He said there was really nothing to be done about it. Some humans wee just plain mean.

The other puppies welcomed me back even though sometimes they thought I was a pain in the behind. Maha held me for a long time. I so wanted to stay with her forever. She had scolded the mean one about her behavior but it did not appear to have any impact on her. That night she went out again! I wondered where her mate was. I woke up one morning and he was gone, but maybe not for long. It was that he was on the other side of the world fighting. That was strange, he was always kind to me.

Pawprints To The Universe

Snuggled with the other dogs and Maha, I got a good night's sleep. Safe and warm. Just the way I like it.

37

Another

Dear Universe,

As much a I like it here with Maha there is always a thought in my mind about another woman. Not sure who she is for I have never seen her. It lingers in my thoughts so I keep looking for her. The mean one left me with Maha, so we had settled into a good routine. The food was good. The outdoor walks were fun. I still wonder about the mother and Blade. Some people think puppies don't have feelings or a memory. We do. I remember every detail of the mother's milk and affection. Blade is running around me trying to bite my tail in most of my dreams. I miss them both but do not have the means to find them. So the only thing to be done is to ask you dear Universe to watch over them. Maybe someday I will find them. Or maybe I will find the woman I seek. That would be good I think.

38

All I Desire Is Love

Dear Universe,

Today is hard because Maha needs to go away and I must stay with the mean one. It's never easy to be around her. She sometimes says nice things but they are usually followed by abuse..... Her anger is something I never understand. Her forgetfulness of my existence is even more baffling. All I desire is love. Hold me. Scratch my ears. Tell me I am your puppy. Anything that bears affection would be nice.

Maha and her kids (the puppies) left early before sun-up. They all were going to a big city they said. Having lived there before, Tory filled me with stories about big city life. I so wanted to go there. With Maha of course not with the mean one. As they pulled away my heart sank. Hoped they would not be like the mother or Blade. Couldn't really bear to even think about it.

The mean one surprisingly put down a bowl of food with water.

"Maha makes you fat", she chided. "So I am only giving you a little bit."

Somehow it didn't matter. I ate it fast, just in case she changed her mind. Before I could get water, she decided she wanted to hold me. That was a switch!

We sat on the couch while she watched the box with people. Tory said it was a television.

Whatever.

The mean one quickly fell asleep. Exhausted from what, I did not know. She was not a cuddle type. I jumped off the sofa hoping to find some extra food while she slept. I wonder where her mate is. Maybe he got another one since she was not so nice. I missed him because he was at least nice to me.

Luckily I found the food bag she left on the chair.

39

The Unseen World

Dear Universe,

I remember the mother telling me about the world. She also told me of the magic of the unseen world. Many people do not know that puppies are very spiritual. The mother's always instill this knowing to their pups at a young age. It made me feel stronger even when circumstances judged me as weak. I survived the disappearance of the mother. I survived the separation from my brother. So far I have survived the mean one. Those are the only bad things. I have met Maha who I know may lead me to the one I am looking for. I can see her in my head. We have known each other in other places. Where? I can't remember. All I know is that she is here somewhere. If I can find her it will be great.

Pawprints To The Universe

I wish I could stash this bag of food somewhere. The mean one often forgets to feed me, so if I had a stash, at least I wouldn't starve.

The moon is high in the sky. Maybe the mother and Blade are looking at it. Maybe they think of me. Maybe the woman is also looking up into the sky.

There are so many maybe's in this place. For once I would like to be sure of outcomes. I don't want to stay with the mean one. Hopefully I can influence Tory to influence Maha to keep me as her own. I would not be a nuisance. Tory seems to think I already am, but he is notoriously picky.

The sun come up and I am going to stay with Maha and the pups. Barks cannot express my happiness. The other pups not so thrilled, but at some point it simply has to be all about me.

40

Still Learning

Dear Universe,

As long as I can stay with Maha and the pups life is pretty good. We go for walks on the beach every day. There is always good food to eat as well. If Maha is doing errands we get to go with her. Riding in the car is fun when you're not by yourself.

I can almost imagine being here forever. The mean one has stayed away. I heard that she was meeting her husband somewhere. Good. Hopefully she will be gone for a long time. I want to stay with Maha forever. I am still learning how to be grown up. Tory and Shannon have helped me a lot. At first I resented them but now understand that they both were just trying to help.

41

Questions

Dear Universe,

It's summertime. Lots of people come to the beach for fun and rest. Maha lives here all the time (even in winter). She used to live in a place called New York. I was born there and rescued by the mean one. Since she likes to go places she now leaves me here with Maha.

Everyone here always says "hi" to me when we go on walks. At first I was uncomfortable with all the attention, but I got over it real fast. It is so good to be loved. Never getting in trouble for peeing indoors cuz Maha always remembered to let me out. Never feeling hungry scrounging for food in the pantry cuz Maha always gave me food with little cheese bits on it. I wonder if she knows how much I love her?

Pawprints To The Universe

Every night I get to snuggle with everyone. I still miss the mother and Blade but this has become my new family. I ask Tory all the time if I will ever know what happened? He said to ask the Universe for answers. So here goes, "Why did the mother not return?" and, "Will I ever see Blade again?"

Tory said Maha would not really know. Most humans did not realize we know and remember so much. They think they are the only ones with family ties.

Looking out the window that night I whispered my questions again. I know you'll tell me the truth dear Universe. I will await your answers. In the meantime the blankets beneath me were soft. Shannon of course was hogging most of the bed. Poor Maha barely had a place to lay with all of us with her. Luckily she did not seem to mind.

42

More Than I Thought

Dear Universe,

So excited! Today I am traveling with Maha to New York. Maybe we can go to the shelter to get the mother and Blade. Shannon, Tory, and I get to go! Very glad that the mean woman is too busy to go. Maybe that is the truth but if not it's okay. All I know is that she is not coming on the trip.

I sat in the back seat with Shannon. Of course Tory sat in the front. He feels he is the patriarch of our little family. So it's all okay. Maha was driving fast but I was able to see some of the great big world. Everyone is going so fast. I wonder if they are all as happy as I am right now? There were other cars whizzing past us. Some of them had other puppies in them, which made me wonder if Blade and the mother might be in them.

Pawprints To The Universe

I know that I should not be hoping for a reunion but I do. Regardless of what humans think, I remember them well while wondering what happened to them. Most humans don't realize how much heart we as puppies have. Maha is the first human who instilled in me a sense of worth that would not have happened without her intervention.

I am glad to know her.

I ask you, dear Universe every day for me to stay here. Right here in this car with my family. I know someday I will move on but it will be forward not towards the mean one. As I watch the road, there is a feeling of freedom. Maybe now I can be more than I thought. There is still that lingering thought of the woman who is my destiny.

43

Manhattan

Dear Universe,

So we are in New York. That's what Maha said it was so I believe her. She also said that this is where the mean one found me. I guess I should be grateful because that all led me to here. That's what I figured out. When the ride in the car is long there is a lot of time to think. Tory says that most humans think we don't think deeply. It makes me laugh to myself when I hear that. Tory also said that if we had different shaped snouts we could talk just like them.

The city was loud. Everyone was in a hurry. I must not remember the early times when I was here. Maha said that this was different because it was Manhattan. Okay, that makes sense.

Pawprints To The Universe

We stayed at a friend's apartment who also had dogs. I kept my snout shut but Tory was complaining that he had to be nice to them. Shannon just wanted a place to lay down. I decided to talk to the two pups that lived there. They wore human clothes while pretending to be big shots. They told me I as a mutt and wouldn't amount to much. It made me sad but then a little mad! I would find my place in the world. These little brats would never be as happy as me. I admit I did yell at them pretty loudly. Maha had to come calm me down. Even she didn't understand why I was so barky. I guess I didn't know either. I apologized as we all went to sleep.

I dreamed of a woman whose smile made me feel like an important puppy….. being with her an accumulation of many times being together. How can you miss someone you haven't met yet?

There was a crashing noise followed by sirens and honking horns. Maha whispered that we should go back to sleep. I felt her hand on my head while instantly relaxing. We were all safe just like the mother did for us so long ago.

Sleep is here. I dream of her again. Will I ever meet her? Or is she just a dream?

44

The Streets Of New York

Dear Universe,

The more I see humans the more I know that most of them are crazy. On the streets of NY we saw all kinds of awful. They yell at each other, throw tantrums, and hurt each other. You name it, they do it. I thought we came to this place to learn stuff. Nowhere did it say we came here to goof off. It looks like the mean humans are always mad, while the crazy ones act silly. What is wrong with all of them?

Tory says there is only one human he trusts and that is Maha. He knows the mean one as well. He says she is not redeemable. That means there is no hope for her behavior.

I always kept up with Tory while walking the sidewalks. Shannon was slower, staying close to

Maha. That gave me a lot of time to tell Tory about the woman I always think about. Was she just something I made up? He said that everyone has a purpose. The Universe always gives pups a chance to make a difference. It made me anxious to be the puppy I came here to be.

Tory said I would find it. He laughed when I told him I wrote you letters in my head.

"You are quite ambitious", he said looking into my eyes.

"Yes. Yes I am".

It was the first time I said it out loud. Maybe I am getting more grown up. Tramping through the streets of New York with Tory is helping me find my way.

"We just have to make sure you don't go back to the mean one", he replied.

"You have to help me!"

Pawprints To The Universe

I stopped right in front of him demanding an answer. The lights turned red so we had to wait. I think Tory felt sorry for me. Maha caught up with us noticing we were having a deep conversation.

"Come on kids, let's go", she shouted.

Tory nipped my ear to move me.

"Don't worry pip squeak, the Universe will think of something."

So dear Universe I am waiting for you to think of something. I can't go back to the mean one. At least let me stay with Maha!

Please!

45

A Good Word

Dear Universe,

Walking the streets of New York I learned a lot. The three of us became a team. Moving together in unison Maha thought we were looking good.

The humans on the other hand not all that great. They drive around in things called cars making noises while screaming and yelling at each other. It makes me wonder if they are like that all the time. Tory who is a seasoned New York pup said he never saw humans be any other way. He figured they were born miserable. With the exception of Maha and a few of her friends, he considered humans just plain mean. That was exactly what the mother had said when we were under the porch so long ago.

Maha took us everywhere. She loved us and was always nice. Tory said he thought she would let me stay with them forever. I'd have to work on being more patient and courteous but he would put in a good word for me.

I feel like I am growing up. I know when to wait and when to move. The streets are becoming more familiar. My roots are in NY so it's no surprise that I have become comfortable. Maha said today that I have become part of her tribe. That makes me happy!

46

Why?

Dear Universe,

Why are humans so mean? Since being in the city I have witnessed some weird events. Most people hate each other I think. They spend no time sniffing the scent. They just dig in with whatever happens. Screaming, yelling and bad behavior is accepted. If I acted like that most likely I would be sent back to the shelter.

In the evenings while settled down for bed, Tory would counsel me about humans. He said that the mother was right. Most of them are just plain mean. We were lucky that our human was Maha. I was even luckier because I got to stay with them so much.

Yeah. I get it. But! But! But! It doesn't answer the question of why? Why are they so mean? Did they have a bad experience that ruined them? Why? If you put us here dear Universe, why did it go so bad for them?

I snuggle into the curve of Maha's leg while dreaming of being with a good human forever. I know she likes me but I still think of the woman I haven't met yet. Keeping the hope alive, that I will.

Sleep overtakes me as I forget all about mean humans. The scent of Shannon and Tory and Maha fill my head with visions of family. The only way it could be better would be if the mother and Blade were here.

Maha says the mean one may show up from time to time, but she would protect me. What a great human she is. I only hope she can pull it off….. the mean one is crafty.

47

The Options

Dear Universe,

OK, the worst has happened. The mean woman has returned claiming ownership of me. Ownership? Oh no. I don't belong to anyone. Tory said that sometimes humans get confused. He is upset as well. He knows that she really doesn't want me.

"What can I do?" I ask.

"Nothing", replied Tory. "Your only hope is that Maha will say no."

I hoped for this so much. With tears in my eyes I left the comfy home of Maha. I sat in the passenger seat of the car staring out the window. So far we have driven further and further away from those I love. The only thing I can do is plot my escape.

We arrived at her house. Of course she had not planned well. There was no food only water. She rummaged around in the kitchen and found some meat which she called hot dogs. What? I was so hungry I at them, all the while wondering if I were indeed eating another puppy.

Would she get some Kibble? Probably not. She wanted me to sleep in her bed but I could not. It made her mad. I ended up in the kitchen on the hard floor. So different than the fluffy bed of Maha. It was cold just like the shelter. I dreamed of being with the mother long ago under the porch. Her warm belly so warm. Her milk so filling. I miss her. Hopefully she is okay. I still hope to see her again.

The ringing woke me up. I heard the woman get up to answer it. I could hear her arguing with someone. Oh please let her stay mad at them and not at me. My tummy is rumbling. The hot dogs all gone. Would she remember to get me some food?

Now I have to pee. Great. I walk into where she is whimpering a bit so she would know.

She was so involved in her conversation she did notice me.

I put my paws on her knees while she sat. The fabric on the arms of the chair was worn thin. For a brief moment I wondered why. It was slippery as my toenails slid right off. Getting her attention was impossible. My bladder was about to burst but her attention was elsewhere.

Trying not to pee was a hard task. My mind raced through the options with myself settling upon the kitchen floor. Experience told me the consequences would be less severe.

Her shrill high pitched laugh echoed into the kitchen as my pee came out. Keeping my paws out of it was no easy task. Under the table it ran submerging into the rug, unfortunately. Maybe it would dry before she noticed. It was her lack of notice that caused the whole mess.

She was still talking when I came back into the room. The couch was soft and inviting so I jumped up to rest. The drone of her voice lulled me to sleep.

Maybe it wouldn't be so bad. Sleep came over me quickly.

48

Be Strong

Dear Universe,

The yelling and screaming right next to my snout brought me back quickly from dreamland.

"You bad dog! How could you be so bad?"

She slapped my snout hard while shoving me off the sofa. I landed on my hip which hurt so much.

Why was she so mad?

I had to pee while she was talking. She did not take the hint to let me out. I did the only thing I could do. I did my business in the kitchen. There was nothing else to do.

"See what you have done you stupid dog? Now I have to clean this up! No! No! No!"

She pushed my face into the liquid. Why do that? If you would just let me outside these things would not happen.

I growled at her for the first time. It surprised her I think. It was time for me to stand up for myself. Tory always encouraged me to be strong.

She grabbed me by the collar while throwing me into a closet. It was dark and cold. Why was I being punished for doing something I could not help.

It's so hard dear Universe. Please. Please get me out of here. I don't know how much more I can take.

49

Why?

Dear Universe,

"What have you done? You are an ungrateful puppy.

"Bad boy!"

"Bad boy!"

I managed to leap off the couch before her hands connected to my snout. She was so mad that I was sure she could have knocked my snout out. Behind the couch I danced back and forth narrowly missing her flailing hands.

Why? Why? Why?

Why was I here with this woman? I thought the world should be a loving place. This had nothing to do with love. So dear Universe, what am I to learn here? I still can't figure it out.

It was dark by the time she stopped yelling. I was safe from her grasp for the time being. My thoughts drifted to Toni and my absent family. Why can I not find my forever home? The image of the woman lingers in the corners of my mind. Will I ever find her? right now it does not seem so.

Despair fills me as my tummy growls with hunger. Maybe I could sneak into the kitchen for a drink of water. My throat so parched it hurts. Peering out from behind the couch there is no evidence of the mean one. Maybe she left again. A shadow darkened the way to the water bowl. If I was sharp I could probably make it there before she found out. Hopefully it would be full of water.

50

Maybe It's Time

Dear Universe,

Things never seem to change. Every day is spent trying to stay out of the mean one's way. Sometimes she leaves me home by myself. It is spent looking for food and trying not to pee or poop in the wrong places. No sign of redemption as I wait for better things. There was talk of visiting Maha and Tory but so far nothing. I wish Maha would keep me with her.

Sometimes I feel like going back to where I came from. Oh Universe, can I just come home to you? Surely where you are is better than this. There is no love here. Just a place where I feel all alone. Maybe it's time to come back to you, Universe….. Maybe it's time.

51

Looking Better

Dear Universe,

Sometimes I think you really are listening to me. Being a small puppy sometimes makes me feel invisible. It's like no one really sees me or cares. You on the other paw found a way to return me to Maha and Tory and Shannon. The mean one decided she wanted to go to the beach for a few weeks. Apparently her family owns a house not far from Maha's. The car could not go fast enough. Even the mean one could not ruin my good mood. She was upset that I wanted to ride in the backseat. She gave up after I jumped back there a bunch of times.

"OK! You little brat", she exclaimed.

"When we get to the beach I'm leaving you at Maha's house so I can have some fun! You'll be sorry you didn't sit up front with me.

Oh dear Universe, I was giddy with excitement. Leaving me at Maha's was the greatest punishment ever!

She was so clueless. Couldn't she see the joy on my face?

So thank you dear Universe for getting me back here. You were right. Things are looking better.

52

Heaven

Dear Universe,

Good News!

The mean one took me back to Maha's house because she said I was a bad boy. Apparently I cause trouble all the time. Gosh, if I knew it would be this easy I would have peed deliberately from the beginning.

I could barely sit still in the front seat of the car. Every time I put my paw on the window there would be a lot of yelling. One is not supposed to put their paws on the car window. Perhaps Maha can help me figure that out.

We pulled in the driveway to find Shannon and Tory sitting on the porch. The sun was out. Tourists were pouring into the little seaside town. Both dogs started barking, prompting Maha to come to the door.

"Welcome home little man!" She bent down to scratch my ears delivering little kisses to my snout. It was heaven.

"I'll keep him for the summer", said Maha. I could barely contain myself. Tory chased me into the house, already irritated with me. Even when he was mad he still loved me, so all was okay.

53

Now Everyone Knows My Name

Dear Universe,

This has been the best summer. Maha is the best human ever! Everyday we go to the beach running all over the place. In the evening we all cuddle up with Maha in bed. She scratches all of our ears while letting each of us hog the bed in our own way.

Tory has taught me a lot. He listened to my idea that there is a special woman out there for me. Maybe he sees it as a way to get rid of me, but I don't think so. Under his thick coat is a wise dog who loves me. Shannon doesn't say much but she does let me have extra blankets at night.

This is the best home I have ever had (except for those early days under the porch with the mother and Blade).

Pawprints To The Universe

When we go for walks I have to keep up with the bigger dogs. I end up running to stay in line with them and Maha. Everyone says "hi" when we walk by. It's so cool that everyone knows my name. The only thing more I would wish for is to find my forever human. I know she exists but where is she? Tory says I have to accept that it might not happen.

54

It's Easier With Love

Dear Universe,

Once she dropped me off I nestled into the sofa in the living room. Just knowing I was gonna get to stay filled me with great love. When the mean one left, the sun began to shine upon me on the couch. The summer ws going to be a good thing. Maha always took me for walks and fed me with much love.

The door slammed and I was free. Maha always tried to love me up when I was there. Just the way she scratched my ears made me feel important.

I was never considered to be he center of attention. Even now I was one of many. There was Tory and Shannon who also lived with Maha. The Shannon liked me a lot. She was always looking out for me. Guiding my choices because I did not really

Pawprints To The Universe

know how to make. Tory was always watching me. I wanted him to like me so bad. Admittedly dear Universe my diplomatic skills are very small. Never knowing how to be in a family I guess it was all an education moment for me. Every time I messed up Tory was there to help me correct my behavior. Little things I found were important. It was a good thing to tell Maha I needed to go outside. It was okay to speak my mind. That had never been an option before. Dear Universe, could this be then my forever home? Maybe the mean one will let me stay here. I do not want to go back. Maha for some reason is trying to placate the mean one. Maybe she will decide to keep me. The vison of the woman remains clear in my head. Maybe I just made it up so I would feel better. The image of her golden hair and hearing the words "Well there is my puppy", stays with me.

The summer continued. My life here filled with joy. The possible reunion with the mean one filled me with dread. I could tell when Maha had spoken with her. She was often in a bad mood in the aftermath. She would tell me she was telling her that I should stay here for the whole summer. Why would the mean one even notice that I was not there?

I wish Maha understood what life was like without her. She needed to keep me with her or I was doomed. I simply could not bear to return to that place with her. Maha told me not to worry and that she would figure something out. In the meantime I continued to dream of my woman who loved me. Was I just making it up? Tory thought so. He encouraged me to forget about the woman. He thought that I should focus on staying with him and Maha. He said Maha loved me and maybe she is the woman I kept seeing. I wanted to believe that indeed this woman was going to show up. If she did I would be forever happy. Tory said take what happiness you can get. Stay here with us, we will find a way to deal with the mean one.

The sun kept us all warm that summer. I was having a great time but there ws a lingering fear that it would all end in the autumn.

At night we all tumbled into bed. I feel for once a connection to all the bodies and felt safe. Part of me wishes Blade was still here to know this feeling. Being a puppy like me was not easy. There were so many things that kept me from my destiny. Maybe being with Maha and her puppies was my destiny. Maybe.

It continued this way through the summer. Filled with love and lots of food, I wanted it to never end. Everyday I could feel the end coming. There was a pebble of fear that simply would not go away. Dear Universe, why? Why am I not able to be secure and happy in this place? Why do I continue to see the woman? Tory says I am a dreamer. If so, why can I not find the woman? It seems so unfair. Something needs to happen but I don't know what it is . Please help me!

Dear Universe, help me find her. I am trying to be a better puppy. It's easier with love, isn't it. Yeah I am figuring that out. With Maha it's all love. The mean one is not sure what love is. She is pretty stuck in her meanness.

I am supposed to go back to her house when summer ends. That's not that far away. It scares me to leave here. If only you could make a miracle happen. Maybe an "angel" could be sent to keep me here where I am loved. I know I will die if I go back there. Hopeless and heartbroken at that thought, I curl up next to Tory. He tells me to suck it up and be a big dog. Well maybe I am not so big. Universe please help me!

55

Summer

Dear Universe,

Time passes while I am so happy at Maha's house. There is a routine, a new word for me, every day. We all get to sleep in Maha's bed. What a great thing that is. I managed to get a spot close to her. I could feel the warmth of all the bodies. It reminded me of being with Blade and my mama. The warmth breath of Tory (Maha's oldest boy) on my face. Once in a while he would snore a little, waking me up. For hours laying in this marvelous cocoon the feeling of love so great. I would nuzzle my snout deep into the covers. If only this were my forever home! There was always the fear that the mean woman would return to claim ownership of me.

I was not really her dog. She did not feed me, walk me, or even love me. She was just plain mean.

Days would pass and just when I thought I was free, she would show up. When she did, it was always a bad day for me. Why? Why dear Universe! Why did this woman claim ownership of me? She never did anything that resembled love. Maha on the other hand taught me what love was all about. I wish I could stay here forever. Maybe she will get bored again and leave. All of my puppy prayers were about my staying in this place forever. I finally found my home. Just had to figure out how to be able to stay here.

It was summer and the summer people were out in full force. In Maha's routine we would eat a great breakfast then go for a walk around the point. The ocean was roaring. The run shining brightly. The sound of laughter everywhere. When I walked with my friends I felt like my life was good. The very hovering of the mean one always lurking in the background. At any time she could swoop in and take me away. The thought of it too devastating to think about. Please dear Universe, let me stay here.

56

Searching For Food

Dear Universe,

So far the summer is good. The mean one has been absent, which makes me very happy. Maha feeds me everyday..... in the morning and at NIGHT! It's so cool that my belly doesn't ache. No one needs to tell me to clean my plate. Sometimes we even get a snack! It's taken a while to get used to it.

Why are some humans so good while others are so mean? Here in Maha's town everyone is nice. I get my own collar/leash when we take our walks (which I found out that's when you're supposed to poop and pee). It's nice to have a schedule to count on. Tory says his whole life has been this way. I told him how lucky he was to have his own human. He said he was glad to share Maha with me. I was happy about that but it still was his human. Not mine.

So I played along with my new family, always looking over my shoulder for the mean one. She always seemed to show up just when I was having the most fun. Every day I looked for my own human. Maha said I could stay forever and that she would try to save me as much as she could. It was bittersweet, but I cling to that hope all the time.

I got to see a lot of humans on our walks. Everyone seemed to know who I am. It's pretty cool to get all the attention. I wonder if any of them know my brother Blade. I keep hoping he will show up as well, but he never does. Hope he's okay wherever he is.

57

Will She Really Be Nice?

Dear Universe,

Boy! You were so right. Life can be great! Living with Tory has been a great life lesson. He's told me how everything works. I find that I am making better choices now. Just yesterday I realized that I have not made any messes here at Maha's. Probably never will cuz she lets me out to the potty. I didn't know humans could be this good. My poor mum must have never met anyone like Maha. For that I feel sorry, for the meeting has made a big difference in my life.

Tory often scolds me but always ends the conversation with a loving head butt. He tells me I'm hopeless but cheers me on when I do something good.

I have found that I love chicken a lot. Sometimes Maha gives me a little extra. She's trying to make up for the mean one I am sure.

The sun was shining on the afternoon that changed my life forever. Maha had been talking to a woman on her telephone a lot. Evidently this woman was going to come for a visit.

Since everyone in Maha's world loved me, I felt warm and fuzzy all the time. Maha said I would have my own on our walks, which meant I did not have to share with Shannon and Tory. So dear Universe, will she really be nice? I hope so. I would dearly love to have my own human even if it was only for a few days. I pretty much had given up on finding the woman I had dreamt about for so long. Maybe it just wasn't for me. If only the mother had come back. If only Blade did not get lost. Life might have been very different. I guess I just need to accept things as they are.

58

Maha's Friend

Dear Universe,

Oh my gosh! Today was an amazing day!

Maha left us at home saying she was going to pick up her friend at the airport. Tory and I snuggled up on the couch. Shannon was on the floor. It seemed like forever she was gone. We all fell asleep and were still asleep when we were awakened by a car engine. We all jumped up so excited! I could see the woman. Her hair was golden and she had a wonderful laugh. I felt like I had heard that laugh before.

The door opened and Maha burst in….. "Hey kids we're back! April is here….."

I sat on the couch in mid-bark. I felt like I was floating on air. This April put her bags on the floor.

Our eyes met..... "Oh look! You have a dog for me!"

She walked towards me while I choked on my bark. She was so beautiful. I wanted to jump all over her, but I stayed on the couch shaking cuz this was the one I was waiting for.

In a mad dash I ran to her. She plopped down on the couch and hugged me. I swear I thought I had died and went to heaven. Yes dear Universe I know it's not a real place but if it were I am sure it would feel like this.

Her scent was perfect. Her hands rubbed my belly in just the right places. I was deliriously in love from the first hello. You told me dear Universe, but I started to not believe you. Boy was I ever wrong.

Her name was April.

Her laughter made me giddy with love. Yes! Love! It had been a long time since I felt like this!

She said "Oh Toni! There's my puppy!"

The words went in my heart and caused it to burst out of my chest. Her arms squeezed me tight. I never wanted to move out of her arms. I was home!

The next few days I never left her side. We ate together. We walked together. We snuggled together all night long. I was obsessed.

Tory laughed at me saying he could see little hearts and flowers floating over my head. He was pleased that April and I had met each other..... finally.

Seeing her brought back to me all the other times we had been together. I could lay my head on her chest feeling her heart beat in unison with mine. I thought of the mother and my brother Blade. Too bad they are lost. They would love my April as well.

The four days went fast. On the morning of departure April sat down with me for a talk. She ws crying. Oh no! Crying was never good in a human. She told me how much she loved me. Maha had told her about the mean one. Squeezing me tightly she told me she wanted me to come with her.

Really?

Where is this place called California?

Where? Where? Where?

She told me it was far far away, but she needed me to go with her or her heart would break. Oh my gosh!! She loved me! This is what I wanted like forever! Of course I would go with her. Tory told me this was my chance to live happily ever after. So the answer was a big whopping yes!

I licked her face so the tears would stop. There was absolutely no one who would be better for me than April. Now she said she just had to figure out how to do it.

My heart was beating real fast when we let for the airport that morning. Snuggled up against her I never wanted to separate. Thankfully the ride was a long one to the Boston Airport. I shut my eyes and pretended to sleep. Maybe she wouldn't go if I was sleeping.

The car stopped and we were there.

No! No! No!

She squeezed me tight and told me that she would be back to get me. No! No! No! I want to go now. Refusing to let go she carried me out of the car.

"Guinness! Listen to me. It's just a short separation! I will be back!!"

That's what the mother said the last time I saw her.

"I'll be back".

She never came back. Maybe April wouldn't either. You told me dear Universe that sometimes things just happen. Maybe the mother couldn't come back. You told me that but now I am understanding it better.

Pawprints To The Universe

Her lips kissed my nose. She laid me back in the seat and was gone.

No. No. No.

59

The Drive Home

The drive home was a sad one. I think I know what it's like to have your soul hurt. Maha asked me to come up to the front with her. Unfortunately I was glued to the back window hoping to get one more glimpse of April. T'was not to be. She disappeared into this place called an airport. She was flying in the air to that faraway place called California. Why could it be that now that I've found her that she would be ripped away from me so quickly. So dear Universe, what can I do? My heart is broke though there is a glimmer of hope that she would come back to get me. Hopefully….. After a while I crawled up to the front to where Maha was. She scratched my ears to soothe me. I just couldn't stop crying.

The mother left me….. Blade….. left me. The only constant was Maha and Tory. Shannon loved me but she was real quiet. Tory told me he had met the April before and that she does come back.

"When!" I cried.

Tory said he wasn't good with the whole time thing but he thought it would be soon. The April always kept her word.

In the meantime I could feel her fingers rubbing my belly. Never had I felt so happy. If only we could run off together forever. I wanted to go to this place called California.

It was a long drive home. The sun had disappeared and I was left in the darkness. There was the bed where snuggled every night while she was here. There was the leash she had clicked on my collar when we went for walks. There was the bowl she touched when she filled it with food. Now her spirit filled the house. How was I ever going to be able to wait for her return?

Tory felt sorry for me so he was extra nice to me in the following days. We went for walks. I ate my dinner but there was this empty place that screamed

April! April! April! How would I ever be able to wait?

Maha reassured me that when April said something she always followed thru. Well I certainly hoped so. Maybe she would be like the mother and never come back. I don't understand dear Universe. Why was I shown this connection only to have it taken away so quickly?

I curled up in the bed we had shared. There was a slight hint of her scent that still lingered on the sheets. I nuzzled my snout deeply into the folds inhaling as much of it as I could. It was all I had left. I know that to grow my spirit I have to endure some difficulty, but this was just too much. How was I ever going to get past this? I did not know.

60

Thank You Universe!

Dear Universe,

Well something bad almost happened. The mean one showed up and wanted to take me to New York. New York? No! No! No! Why? Universe please tell me, why? She doesn't love me.

Maha saw my panic and gently patted my head. She told her it would be better if I just stayed with her. That having a dog with her would cramp her style.

I closed my eyes begging you dear Universe to save me. I watched her face hoping she would agree. Her lips twitched a bit as she stared at me.

Yeah! "I think you're right Maha. I will leave him here. No need to cramp my style!"

I leaped out of the chair and ran to Maha. She scooped me up while whispering, "See wee one? You get to stay with me! Yay!"

The mean one left the next morning. Thank you Universe! Finally things are more secure….. at least for now.

We were in the end of summer. There were still a bunch of people enjoying the warmth and sunlight. I was popular. I had good food. Everyone likes me. I am loved. What more could a pup like me need? Really nothing. I was suddenly blessed but I still did not have my own human. Tory said sometimes you just have to settle with how things are. I should be thankful for what I did have. No worries. Stop reaching for my own human. Be satisfied with what you have. His words kept repeating in my head.

I tried dear Universe, but always found myself looking longingly at other puppies with their human. Maha belonged to Shannon and Tory. I was lucky to be a part of that. So I accepted my fate hoping to extend my visit with my surrogate family.

I still kept my eyes open though.

61

No. No. No.

Dear Universe,

It's been a few weeks since the April left. I keep watching in the window awaiting a car to drive up. It would be glorious if it would be her but it never was. Maha said she had talked to her and she was making arrangements, Gosh, how long would that take?

Yes dear Universe I know I am an impatient puppy. It's so cruel to let me find her and then she goes away. I know that those you love the most sometimes don't come back. It was starting to look that way.

It was dark one night when we all heard a car pull up. The head lights glared into the front window. Of course Shannon, Tory and I reacted in our usual protective way. I thought I saw a woman emerge from the car. Oh! was it her? Was it the April?

No.

It wasn't.

It was the mean one arriving for a surprise visit. No No No!!

"Hi Guinness! It's me, your mama!"

Oh no!

You are not my mama! I ran upstairs hoping to escape her clutches. She ran up the stairs grabbing me from behind.

On no.

She put her face right in mine. "Oh Guinness! Look at you! Maha has been feeding you too much. Look how fat you are!"

My heart fell quickly. Her hands feeling rough as she stroked my fur.

Oh no.

This is the worst thing to happen. "I've come to take you back to New York with me! Aren't you excited?" No. No. No.

Once again Maha saved me by saying, "No! You will leave him here." Thank god! She left without me.

62

Two Weeks

Dear Universe,

The weeks following her departure were sad and bleak. I know that the Universe wants me to be happy but how can I do that when the love of my life goes away? It brings up the loss of the mother and Blade. I know I should be trusting but the whole life has been about loss. It was time for it to be about love. At least that is what you always told me.

Maha comforted me as much as she could. Tory got tired of my whining and told me to suck it up.

Suck it up?

I was really mad at him. His whole life had been with Maha. She was the right human match for him and Shannon. He never had to put up with a mean one of any kind. I know he's only trying to help but

I just want my April back. Would I really get a happily ever after like Tory and Shannon? I didn't know. Being so scared that I would lose her, I probably was a little needy.

Maha said she talked to my April and that she was making arrangements to bring me to California. May as well be the moon. All I really wanted to know was when.

Every day I sat in the window hoping that that would be the day she would pull up in front of the house. Every day Maha would scratch my ears while telling me to be strong because my April ws coming to get me.

Sigh…..

It's been like forever. Sometimes I think she may forget me. The mother and Blade loved me too. They, however, never came back. What if April doesn't come back? Being with Maha was great, but she wasn't my forever human. Tory said I needed to be strong and that he was sure I could stay with them until she came back.

Pawprints To The Universe

Sinking down into the blankets I began to believe him. This family could be just as good..... couldn't it?

I was confused and worried. The leaves on the trees began to fall. Every day I went for walks around the point. The waves crashing with little misty sprinkles made my fur get wet. I never got in trouble for anything. Maha, Tony, and Shannon were my home for now. If only I can hold out until the April returns.

All was well until Maha sat me down for some news. She paused briefly, which made me scared. "Honey I have some bad news", she said.

My heart stopped beating for a second as she told me she needed to take a trip.

"Oh! When are we leaving?" I asked. The silence told me everything. I wasn't to go with her, but I was going somewhere.

Where?

I watched her eyes as she said, "You will have to stay with the mean one for a few weeks while I am gone."

Her eyes looked sad but I could feel that she did not have a choice. Shannon and Tory were staying elsewhere.

Why?

Why?

Why?

I can feed myself. If you leave the door open I could just stay here.

Couldn't I?

Apparently not. Tomorrow we are going to a house in New York.

New York!

How could Maha allow this to happen. My April would rescue me. I was certain. She would come and get me while stopping the mean one. Maha hugged me tightly but said that this would be the last time it would ever happen.

What if Maha never came back? I cried myself to sleep that night. Pulling the blanket close I felt the warmth of Maha and the dogs. Why dear Universe do I have to go? She doesn't love me at all. There will be two weeks of no food, no comfort, no Maha, no Tory and Shannon, but the worst of it was no April.

How would she ever find me in New York?

The sun came up the next day while Maha drove me to New York. It felt like I was going to my death. Images of the mother filled me. What had really happened to the mother? Did she just forget or did something bad happen? Tory said I was whining too much. "Just suck it up! The time will pass quickly. The very worst that will happen is that you will come back to Maine with us".

Easy for him to say.

I wish he would stop saying that.

The car pulled up in front of the mean one's house. My heart was pounding so hard. I tried to look relaxed but I was screaming on the inside. Maha had tears in her eyes as she led me into the house.

There she was in the kitchen. I did not see a water or food bowl anywhere. This was going to be hard. Maha kissed me and said she would be back as soon as she could. She promised.

63

Time Passed

Dear Universe,

She promised to come back. It is the only thing that I had to hang onto. The mean one did not disappoint. She began her tirade as soon as Maha left. I found a familiar hiding place under the bed. Setting up camp amongst the dust bunnies was all too familiar. Would there be any chance she would put down water and food? The preparation for the deprived days ahead seemed daunting. Dear Universe can I just come home? Back to where you are? The earth is where you are? The earth is not a friendly place. There are few humans that have hearts. The rest of them are like the mean one. I feel like giving up. Yes my April has appeared but she left so soon. I am so not sure I can be ok if she doesn't come back. Please give me a sign that I can make it through the next few weeks. Right now my tummy is growling and my tongue so dry. The mean one is still here I think. What will I do if she doesn't give me nourishment.

Time passed as I fell asleep in the safety of the underbed. There was no sound in the house. Maybe it was safe to come out.

Oh!

I just remembered that maybe she left the toilet open. Wow! Maybe I could at least get water.

Slowly I stepped into the hallway. Nope. No mean one.

A quick trot to the bathroom was successful. She had left the top up! I managed to quench my thirst. The best part about the toilet was that it always had water. Now I was pretty sure I cold stay alive.

I reached the kitchen. It was confirmed. I was indeed alone. No sign of a food or water bowl.

64

The Hope

Dear Universe,

The sun has come up many times since I was brought here to the mean one. The only thing I live for is the hope that some how my April will find me. At the very least there was the addition of hope that Maha would return.

What am I supposed to learn here? I know that I am destined to be with my April forever. So why does it have to be such a long wait? I feel like a puppy again waiting for the mother to return. I know that the situation is different but I still feel the loss of the mother and of course my brother Blade.

Every day was a battle to get food and water. The mean one solely focused on herself would often forget the basics. I tried to remind her but sometimes she would just ignore me. Tried to hold my pee and poop but was often derailed by nature. Please dear universe let my April or Maha come back to get me. Not sure how long I can survive here.

65

Hope

Dear Universe,

I was on the back of the couch looking out the window. As usual hoping for rescue. I watched the clouds float by wondering what little guy like me was doing here? I know you told me life is full of lessons but I have already had my fair share. I think if I could become the puppy who belongs to the April then maybe there is hope for me after all. I promise to be a good boy (well, I will try) at all times. Looking every day for my April to rescue me. It's been more than the few weeks Maha said it would be. If she doesn't come back like the others can I just come home back to you dear Universe?

Every car that goes by my tail begins to wag with excitement. So far all the cars pass me by. Will I ever see them again? Feeling sad and worried this day.

66

My Beloved Family

Dear Universe,

Yay! Today Maha came back! Never have I been so happy to see anyone! Jumping into her arms I never wanted to leave there.

"Are you okay G?" she whispered. All of the bad stuff of the past few weeks just fell away. The mean one stared at me with anger. I guess it was because I did not feel the same way about her.

"What about me G? Don't you want to be in my arms?' said the mean one.

Maha turned away from her quickly allowing me to escape her clutches

"Just get me out of here Maha! Please let's just go!"

I was in the car with my beloved family so fast that I was elated. Tory in the back seat even moved over so I would have space.

"I hear your gonna stay with us for a while!" Yep! Maha tells me "It's just until the April come from California to get you!"

My April was coming to get me? It was the end of October, which really meant nothing to me. Not sure how humans measure what they call time. All I knew was that she was coming. Maybe as soon as tomorrow.

"No. I heard it was in December". Tory was far more worldly than me. I was wondering how you created that dear Universe. The world is so big!

We walk around the point and sometimes the waves go so high a little guy like me can get scared. Tory however always walks between me and the water. He said he was bigger so he would protect me.

Sigh…..

It's so great having a big brother. I so really wanted to believe him.

"Are you sure!? When will it be December? Tomorrow?"

Tory told me he wasn't' sure. The whole time marking thing was always way too complicated for me.

So as I sat in the back seat with Shannon I dreamed of my April coming to get me. She would be back. Everyone said so….. so it must be true.

It was glorious to be back home with Maha. The tourists had all left by now. It was just a few people left for the winter. Every day I would watch the front window hoping to get a glimpse of my April. It was now coming up to November. A few more weeks until she would come to get me. Maha took us for walks every day. The ocean is so big and wild.

67

Thanksgiving

Dear Universe,

Well. I am still waiting. There was a holiday where all the humans thank you for everything. Here are the things I am thankful for. I am thankful for.....

Walks around the point.

Breakfast and dinner every day.

Getting a chance to poop and pee in the right places.

Not getting yelled at or hit.

Shannon's warm belly that sometimes she lets me close to keep warm.

Maha's kisses.

Knowing my April is coming soon.

The days are peaceful but I am full of excitement as December gets close. If I could just manage to remember how many days 'til them, but I cannot.

Every day Maha tells me my April is coming to get me. She says that I am going to the place called California. I don't know where that is but maybe it's near where the mother and Blade disappeared. Boy would that be so cool. I wonder if Blade will remember me. Tory says I dream too much. I don't think so. Without my dreams I would have despaired of the life long ago

So dear Universe, I am beginning to understand how important it is to have dreams. Just never thought I could actually make them happen. Is that part of the lesson of becoming a better puppy? I think it is. It's a great feeling to know that the Universe is on my side. Did not know that when I was younger.

So I sit in the window while waiting for my April to show up. Maha loves me but she has her own puppies. I would have to share with the others and I really want to, but I also need my own human. That is my April.

68

Just Another Mystery

Dear Universe,

It's me….. Guinness! Next week my April is coming to get me. Maha said she was flying through the air. Wow, I never knew humans could fly! It's so cool!

Tory told me I needed to reconnect with you Universe. He said this new connection and adventure was really a great moment for me. He said you were proud of me. Are you dear Universe? If you are, it would be so cool.

Maha and my April talked a lot on the telephone. It always surprise me that California was so far away but so close on a telephone. Just another mystery that probably has no answer. All I know is that I am going to California with my true love….. April.

69

On My Way

Dear Universe,

Today is the day! Maha put a new collar on me and patted my head.

"You're going to California little man!" she said.

Oh wow.

Was I gonna fly in the air? It was scary to think about that. I've seen birds fly but never thought I could grow wings to do it. I guess I was wrong. Kept looking at my reflection in the window. No sign of feather growth. So I really did not understand how I was gonna pull it off.

Tory just laughed at me. "Guinness! Stop being so stressed about this! Trust the April that she will get you home with her. From what I hear, you are not flying".

Not flying? How was I gonna get there without flying? So much to worry about. I admit I had a bit of a melt down. Maha held me close but I did bark a lot while running up and down the stairway.

Soon it ws time to go to the airport. I jumped in the car into the back seat. Tory was up front while Shannon snoozed beside me. I hoped that Maha would go real fast. It was an airport. Boston Airport. I thought it would be a quick ride followed by a fast reunion. Boston though was far away. Maha told me to sit back and relax.

Relax?!!!

I am on my way to the love of my life! I'm gonna go to California and be with her for the rest of my life. I am such a lucky puppy. The ride to meet up with her is endless. Dear Universe, how do I bend time to go faster? Is there such a thing?

70

April's Perspective

My friend Toni and I have known each other over 30 years. She used to be my talent agent. I grew out of being just a talent, moving on to working for Toni's New York based agency. I became the West Coast manager for corporate events and Marvel Comics.

Toni and I found that we had a lot in common. Over the years we also became close over the dogs we owned and rescued.

In the summer of 2006 Toni had vacated New York to move permanently to Maine. It was a big decision for her but she had vacationed there over the years, having the calmer energy she has become more attracted to.

Pawprints To The Universe

It was late that summer that I made a visit to Toni right before Labor Day. The trip would change my life forever.

Toni picked me up at the Boston Airport. The trip to Biddeford was about a two-hour trip. Both of us were excited to spend some time together. I had heard so many wonderful stories about the beach. Toni and her dogs (Shannon and Tory) were like a second family to me. An image of us going for walks around the point filled my thoughts on our journey to Toni's house.

We arrived without incident. Toni had filled me in about Guinness. He apparently really belonged to Toni's niece Helene, but Toni kept him as often as she could. She said he had some emotional issues around his treatment by Helene. Toni said she never should have acquired a dog. There was a disconnect with her treatment of him. Thus Toni "baby sat" him often.

As we pulled in the driveway I could hear dogs barking. I loved Shannon and Tory, knowing them in New York City. Now they were "country dogs". I couldn't wait to scoop them up in my arms.

I remember clearly that entrance. Dropping my bags I expected a hug from Shannon and Tory. What I got was a little black dog who charged at me at great speed. He jumped into my unprepared arms so fast I almost fell over. "Wow! There's my puppy! You got one for me to walk too!"

His little nose was warm. His little tongue kissing my nose and cheeks. He was quite the little lover. His anxiety was evident as he could not settle down in my arms. I sat in a chair to get stable, then hugged him to me tightly. His heart started to beat in unison with mine. His body relaxed in my lap. I swear it felt so familiar. It was quite a meeting, one that I will never forget.

Toni immediately announced that we were going to go on a walk around the point. She grabbed three leashes, throwing one at me for Guinness. I struggled to clip it on but once I did, Guinness looked me right in the eyes. I was hopelessly in love from that moment on.

We started walking, which was a bit clumsy. Guinness kept running into Shannon because he was looking over his shoulder at me.

I have to admit that it was one of the cutest things I had ever seen. All I wanted to do was pick him up and hug him. Our first walk around the point felt so natural. It was like it was not our first encounter. That was silly I thought. He was a young boy so meeting him earlier was impossible on so many levels. However here I was, in love with a puppy I barely knew.

Night came swiftly. Toni had set up a bed in the little alcove in her upstairs. After flying all day, coupled with jet lag, I was eager for some sleep.

I recall laying down, pulling up the covers. Within seconds there was Guinness flopping himself down next to me. He nuzzled his nose while licking my face. Toni called for him but he had already decided where he was going to sleep. I have to say I was thrilled.

Pawprints To The Universe

He wriggled up the blanket laying his head on my chest. Our hearts again were beating in unison. I fell asleep content and peaceful.

In the morning he was bouncing all over the place. I heard him giggle while playing under the sheets. I called his name.

"Guinness".

His little snout appeared followed by his big brown eyes. They appeared to see right through me. I heard distinctly…..

"Oh boy! So you wanna be my human? I've been wanting one for so very long. Maha said she'd do it but she is already taken by Shannon and Tory. Be my human! Be my human. Pretty please! Be my Human!"

His tongue licked my face causing me to agree to anything this little fur ball wanted. While I was putting his leash on he ran back and forth between myself and Maha. He looked so excited I could hear him repeat over and over….. "My April". It was magical.

For the rest of the trip we were inseparable. We hung out, ate food, did long walks. He was at my feet when Toni and I played Scrabble. It was as if we had always been together. Nothing was awkward. It was smooth, subtle, and satisfying. I never wanted to be separated from him again.

Maha in her wisdom could see clearly what was going on. It must have been cool to witness a developing love affair. For that's what it turned out to be.

On the last day of my trip the harsh reality of separation began to reveal itself. I was leaving for California. It was thousands of miles away.

I spoke to Maha expressing my deep sorrow at leaving Guinness behind. The thought of it brought me to tears.

Maha suggested that something could be done, but it need to be planned out. It was in this conversation that bringing G to California was going to be the plan.

We sat up late trying to figure out a way. Since time was short, bringing him back on the airplane seemed to be the only option. In the morning we made a few calls, only to find there were already dogs in the cabin of my returning flight.

The cloud of sadness about having to leave him to return to California hovered over my head the last day. The ride to the airport devastating. I held G on my lap while he leaned into me. Our hearts were beating in unison. I told him the separation was necessary for now, but I would arrange something as quickly as I could.

Toni pulled to the curb while my heart sank. I hugged him close while dragging myself out of the car. His little tongue licked my face frantically. He knew what was coming. We both did. I braced myself for the final hug. Toni grabbed my suitcase from the back of the car. A quick hug and then it was time to say goodbye.

I asked Toni how could this have happened so quickly. I wanted to stuff him in my suitcase. I waved with tears in my eyes as they drove away. Guinness had jumped into the back seat barking his head off. His little nose pressed against the window was heart breaking.

I think the walk into the terminal was one of the most devastating moments of my life. His scent was still on my shirt. Images of his eyes looking at me haunted the whole flight home.

I was determined to get G here with me in California. The mission was in full force in my head. Upon landing I was armed with information on how to get Guinness home with me.

My first call upon landing was to Toni….. to ask how my puppy was.

71

Later Perspective Of April

During the latter part of September that year I got busy finding how I was gonna get Guinness to California. At first I thought I would just fly him out. I soon found out he was too big and heavy to fit under the seat. This was a big red flag for me. A few years before I was witness to a dog that had flown in baggage. Something went wrong and the poor puppy came down at baggage claim deceased. Apparently there was a problem with oxygen and cabin pressure on that particular flight. After that experience, no way was I going to fly him to California.

So I was left to find other ways to accomplish this task of love.

My next thought was to simply drive across the country and pick him up and drive back. That idea was shot down by those who loved me, especially my husband Allen. They all felt that a woman driving alone cross country was just not a good idea. So back to the drawing board.

During this time Toni had business that required her to travel. Bad news for Guinness because he was to be left with Helene (Toni's niece) for two weeks in New York. I was flabbergasted and worried. I knew that Toni had no other choice but boy was I scared.

Poor G.

The only thing I could hope for was that the time would go fast. I didn't think Helene would harm him physically, but I know more emotional damage was coming his way.

I was relentless trying to find a way to solve this transportation problem. Getting Guinness in my arms became an obsession. Even my friends were surprised at the intensity behind my quest.

After hours of research I finally found a pet transport that delivers pedigree dogs that were purchased out of state to their new owners.

They offered delivery across the country and more. Three guys. One drove, one slept, and one took care of the animals. By doing it this way, they were able to deliver cross country in about three days. They allowed you to keep track of the journey though their website. The would also provide photos and updates along the way. To me, it was the perfect solution. The whole thing cost about $600. A lot of money for me at the time, but I was completely driven to get Guinness to me in California.

I called Toni with excitement. She was thrilled to have a solution. Together we decided that the beginning of December I would fly back to Maine to put him on the transport. When he arrived in Los Angeles I would be at the other end to receive him.

Toni said she was picking G up from Helene the next day. No more business trips. She would keep G under her loving care until it was time to board the transport.

I was relieved. I just hoped that Helene had not done more damage to my little guy. It was going to be a long emotional recovery for him. I was up for the task.

The next day Toni successfully picked up Guinness. For that I was relieved. Now it was just a countdown until December 6th.

72

So Many Questions

Dear Universe,

We sat at the airport for a very long time. Maha said the flight was delayed. How can that be? Sometimes all this human stuff is so hard for a puppy like me. Why are humans so in a hurry but seem to go nowhere? It seems to me that if they just sat still for a moment they would do better. Sometimes being a puppy is a difficult thing. We need to have our own human I think. One that loves us so much they would never ever yell at us.

Just knowing my April was coming to see just me was enough for me to cry. Most humans don't know we can be sad. I have heard so many times that I am just a dog and what do I know? Well maybe there's a lot of things I don't know but one thing is for sure. I am a lucky puppy. I now have my April and I am going to fly back to California in the sky real soon.

How does flying when you are a puppy work? Will I get some feather wings like the birds I see here at Maha's?

So many questions in my head. Sitting here in the airport I can barely breathe let alone fly. Tory said it would all work out. He said that you told him it would.

How do you know dear Universe? I heard that sometimes there is a crystal ball that tells the future. Maha has a ball but it's not crystal. Sometimes she throws it for Tory and I. Shannon always says no thanks, but we feel compelled to chase it and bring it back to Maha. I've never seen a ball that you could look into. Is it really something? Or is it just a stupid story that sometimes gets told?

There was a voice that spoke out loud that a human had just landed. Well they said a plane but I am not sure what that is. Maybe my April would be tired from all that flying. Maybe I should be watching for her.

Maybe.

Maybe.

Maybe.

And then….. there she was! I froze for a second. She was smiling as she stooped down to my level.

"GUINNESS!" she screamed.

I thought my heart ws going to beat out of my chest. If only Blade was here to see this! I jumped into her arms and that was that. I was home at last.

The April was crying, which she said were tears of joy. Her wet face nuzzled into mine. I thought I was going to explode with happiness.

You were right dear Universe, this time the mother returned. I could feel the sadness leave me. It felt so good. I realized that her abandonment scarred my heart a lot. Now it was healing while nestled in the arms of my April. I couldn't stop given her kisses. They were originally intended for the mother who never returned. I spent so much time grieving the abandonment that I never considered that maybe the mother could not come

Pawprints To The Universe

back. As I licked the face of the April I could see why she never came back. She was run over by one of those big wagons called cars. Oh my god! I never considered that! Why didn't I figure that out? Well I was very young and just starting to connect with you at that time.

I think I feel a little mad that you never told me what happened to the mother. I suffered with that knowledge for a long time. Now since you revealed the true story, I feel a lot better. You said I wasn't ready to know everything at that time. I guess you're right. If it had been explained, maybe I never would have been at Maha's and I never would have met my April. Oh! It's so confusing but I do know that my little heart is already starting to heal. I guess I won't stay mad at you dear Universe.

73

The Doggie Store

Dear Universe,

It was a big surprise that we all went to the doggie store. I had only been there once before with the mean one. That time I accidently pooped on the floor of the store. She was so mad at me! If she had just given me a chance to go outside I would have. She dragged me in so fast I couldn't get it out until we stopped inside the store. You remember that too dear Universe? She dragged me out to the car smacking my behind as I jumped in the car. It was all so terrible. I never thought I'd see the doggie store again but here I am!

The April put me in a cart while she pushed me up and down the aisles. I felt like a prince. I smiled at everyone. Someone even said I was a cute puppy. Me? Cute? You told me I was beautiful but no human (besides Maha) ever did. So I stood up with my paws on the edge of the cart. I was riding high on this trip to the store. Everyone was looking at me. For the first time I actually felt beautiful!

Then April bought some stuff for me, announcing that tonight I was leaving for California. I was so excited but I ws sure that she was going with me. When we got back to Maha's house she gave me a bath. It was warm and the touch of her hands was the best thing ever. She wrapped me in a blanket holding me close to her for a long time.

Maha and the April said that I was gonna go on an adventure but it ws going to be by myself.

By myself?

Dear Universe? Why by myself? Especially after the April came all the way here?

The April held me close whispering the huge plan that was made to get me to California. They had arranged for three guys to drive me there. It was very safe. One guy drives, one guy sleeps, and one guy takes care of the passengers. It sounded okay but it was already dark and I did not see any trucks or transports. The April rubbed my belly while I dozed off. Dreams of being with her in other places danced before me. To have met up with her again is a true miracle. I suppose I owe it all to you dear Universe. By myself I never would have had the courage or the will to keep living. You let me to Maha who led me to the April. It's possible I never would have found her without your help. I am forever a grateful puppy. If you could, there is one thing missing. My brother Blade is still missing. Is there any way you could find him? It would be so cool to have him go to California with me. I hear it's warm and there is lots of food. Way better than that leaky wet porch we used to hang out under. I want him to experience all this love. Wherever he is I'm sure he misses me too. It was the only sad thought that eventful night. I could still feel his furry body next to mine under that porch. If only he has been as lucky as I have been then I would feel better. Please dear Universe when I am ready please let me know where he is and if he is okay.

74

Good Bye

Dear Universe,

Oh boy. What a night. We fell asleep on the couch for a little while. She held me so close I felt like we had become one. Tory said I was snoring but it felt more like I was purring and I'm not a cat!

The April woke me up saying it was time to go. Time to go? In the middle of the night?

We got in the car without Shannon and Tory. The April held me close making me feel safe. It was also scary because I could feel the tension in the car as we drove.

What was going on?

Both Maha and the April told me that they were taking me to a transport that would take me to California?

What? By myself? I wasn't sure if I was brave enough to go by myself. She said it would be okay and that she would be there to pick me up on the other side.

Ok.

Ok.

I will be brave.

Well dear Universe I was brave until the car stopped in a parking lot. There was a huge truck there. Three guys got out of it when we pulled up. They all smiled and said "hi" to me. I sniffed them finding that their scent was okay..... thank you dear Universe for reminding me to do that.

The April hugged me close while whispering her love in my ear. Before I knew it I was in the truck. I was put in a crate with a huge fluffy pillow. The door clicked shut as I realized I was a prisoner. The panic rose up in me. I started to bark hysterically. Where were you dear Universe? I had finally everything I ever wanted….. my own human. In a rush of energy I yelled that I am not a hostage! Where was I going? Was it to another place like California, or was it California? My poor puppy brain was filled with treachery. The April came back only to send me to my doom! Oh no! Dear Universe please, please, please, help me.

"Hey little fella….. are you okay?" One of the three guys was looking through the bars of the crate. His voice was soft. His eyes looked kind but since I have been fooled before I just kept barking at him. If they were going to hurt me I would go down kicking and barking.

The truck was shaking a bit because it was moving. The nice guy opened the cage door. Realizing that this might be my only chance to escape, I lunged forward at the first opportunity. I could bite him hard and then I could finish the other two off before they would realize what was happening. Then I could run back to Maha and the April. It occurred to me that they might have been fooled by this plot as well.

"Hey little fella! Come here, let me hold you for a while".

Hold me? For what reason! He reached in and pulled me out. I was prepared to fight to the death. It was a shock that his hands were soft. His sweater smelled nice. His voice so soothing.

"You are going to be fine. My name is Tom. The other guys are Bradley and Steve. We are taking you to your new home in California. Nothing bad is happening. You just need to settle down to sleep. I'll hold you until you feel better".

Feel better? I wanted to believe him. I was in fact very sleepy. The fluffy pillow was mine. Suddenly I relaxed against Tom who was convincing. He gave me a cookie while he scratched my ears. This wasn't so bad after all.

So I decided to go with your advice dear Universe. Even if you've been betrayed it's important to heal yourself to be able to trust again.

At first I thought you were wrong! Once burned, always burned, that's what the mother always told me. She always said you couldn't trust humans.

Was I being foolish by deciding to do so? Would I see my April at the other end like she said? So many questions as I was put back on my fluffy pillow. Dreams of being held kept me feeling safe.

75

Two Meals A Day, Plus Snacks!

Dear Universe,

I woke up to meet Bradley. He said that it was his turn to take care of me. He fixed some food that tasted funny. At first I did not want to eat it in case it was poison or something. I was so hungry so I ate it anyways. It was better than the bugs under the porch.

The truck had stopped shaking and the door in the back opened. Bradley told me it was time for a walk. I could poop, pee, and stretch my legs all at once. I was relieved as I was about to poop/pee in my crate. Other times I would have got in trouble for doing so. Bradley understood that I need to go out to do so.

So cool! A human who understood. Maybe life was changing for the better after all.

We walked in a park that had squirrels. I had been chasing after them. Bradley ran to keep up with me, which was really cool!

It smelled so different here wherever this was. Maybe they were taking me to another galaxy. I know you use that word a lot, but it's the first time I ever used it. I think I am growing up. Everyday I feel better about living. This ride in this truck was odd but if the end will put me with my April, then I was ready to go.

Bradley put me back in the crate. I found a sock that smelled familiar. After a few sniffs I realized that it smelled of Maha and my April and Maha's house. It gave me the image of being in my April's arms.

Whew!

I am sleepy.

I just ate breakfast. Bradley says puppies should have two meals a day, plus snacks!

Wow!

Wish Blade was here. He would love having all this food. I wonder if he got on a truck like this? Maybe that's why I never found him. I wish every day he was here..... Maybe someday I will see him again.

In the afternoon I finally met Steve. I think he was the nicest. He scratched my ears and let me sit on his lap. When we made a stop he took a picture of me. He said it was for my April. That she wanted to see how I was doing?

Really!

Where is she?

When you gave her a picture does that mean she can see it from where she is? So confusing.

Steve said he sent it to her. He showed me this box thing that had stuff moving around. The only other time I had seen one was at Maha's house. Maybe she could see me too.

I puffed out my chest so they would know I was okay. The truck started up again taking me ever closer to California.

I closed my eyes and remembered all you have ever told me. Never would I have imagined that this would be my experience. I started as an unwanted puppy, my future bleak at best. For all the troubles that began with the mean one, I am still here. Will I make it to California? You've told me all the love coming my way. I did not believe you at first. I thought it all a lie until now. Hope the search for my April will not be forgotten. I want to be close to her forever.

The hum of the truck rocks me to sleep. I feel the cushion under my chin as Steve plays some soft music. It is way different than the music the mean one played. I was driving to California. My April was going to meet me. My eyes grow heavy with a full belly. Steve said time would go quicker if I took a nap. Maybe he was right. I liked him a lot. He never yelled at me ever. I know sometimes I can be a pain in the butt. Tory says I might never grow up to be a smart puppy. But he is wrong. I am making smart choices now all the time. Tory says I need to behave myself. Ok I will. Chances to be happy should always be taken. You told me that dear Universe. Now I know it's true.

76

Home

Dear Universe,

The truck stopped vibrating with movement abruptly. It woke me up with a jolt. What was happening? I could not see out the window, having been all snuggled into my pillow. It felt safe like under the porch when Blade and I had huddled there so long ago.

The truck made funny noises as it came to a stop. The back door was slowly opened. There was no sun shining. It was pitch black, no light at all.

Where were we?

Was this California?

Where was the April? My April?

Maybe it was a mistake?

My caretakers all assembled in front of my sleeping crate. "Come on Guinness! You are home little buddy!"

Each one of them held me briefly while squeezing me in a huge hug! They were cool dudes..... all three of them. I was distracted trying to see where my April was.

"Was she here?"

Did she know I was here?

In the darkness I could hear footsteps on the gravel getting closer. Was it her? I was wriggling in Steve's arms. His fingers gently stoking my ears. If my April did not show up I could settle for Steve in his arms.

"Hey buddy", he whispered. "Here comes your mom!" said Steve.

I turned my head while spotting her gold hair running towards me. "Guinness", she cried.

I jumped out of Steve's arms into the hug of my April. Her face nuzzled into mine. My heart was about to burst out of my chest! She was here!

I could hear a man's voice thanking my three new friends. His name was Allen. Apparently he was related to my April somehow. Right now all I could do was lick her face. Her arms held me close. I was home.

What did home look like? Would it be like under the porch with the mother and Blade? I didn't know. It was a long time ago. Far away, practically on a different planet.

Now I was in the arms of my April walking up a nighttime path to my new life. A new beginning. A new world. In the distance I could see a light. My April whispered in my ear that we were almost there. Almost home. I wondered what Blade would think. He's probably the only puppy I could share this reunion with. He would have loved this. Warm hugs, lots of food and the breath of my love on my neck.

She said it was really early so the sun would not come up for a while. She said, "Lets go upstairs to snuggle 'til it's light outside".

Of course I was in agreement. I couldn't wait to get under the covers. I remember how the stairs creaked as she took me upstairs. It was heaven.

The bed was fluffy and warm. Her arms around me reassuring and comfy. What luck to find this woman and for her to love me back!

She said "Come on! Get under the covers quick!"

I almost fell all over myself as I raced to snuggle in. Covers pulled up as I circled into my April. My back against her belly as we "spooned". At least that's what she called it. Wasn't sure what exactly a spoon was but with all the other new stuff I was sure to find out at some point.

77

Thank You Dear Universe

Dear Universe,

My April slept with her arms around me. It was heaven to be so loved. I could hear her breathing just like Blade used to when I laid with him under the porch.

From the bed I could see the outside getting brighter with sunlight. It was like my new life was beginning with bright light. Could that have been you dear Universe just saying "hi!" I hope so. I closed my eyes determined not to break the magic spell that seemed to be in play. Blade used to say I was too heavy when I laid on him. The April was under me. I could actually hear her heart beat.

Thank you dear Universe for being so patient with me. Without you I might not have survived with so much hope.

78

Eros and Tempest

Dear Universe,

I must have slept for days. The only thing that could wake me up was my hunger pains. I had, however, learned to ignore those signals especially when there was no hope of any food. Today, however, was different. All I had to do was lick my April's face once. She looked at me with a smile. There was no resentment or anger. There was simply an unsaid agreement that breakfast was coming.

"I'll be right back", she said. I trusted her but the mother had said the same thing and she never came back. So naturally I was terrified.

Jumping off the bed I followed her to the door. She patted my head, then was gone. My heart sank. What if she didn't come back? The thought was too much to bear. It was scary to jump off the bed but I had to follow her to wherever she was going. I also started to cry at the thought of being left alone again.

"Stay right here Guinness", she whispered.

It was so hard to say okay. I kept my snout at the base of the closed door trying to keep her in my sight. It seemed like an eternity.

I looked around the room hoping to find a way downstairs to her. I guess my crying helped bring her back. Her feet on the stairway was a welcome sound. As the door opened I could smell it. A different smell than I ever smelled.

"Here's some chicken my little man", she said as she sat the plated down.

I couldn't believe it! Was this all for me?

I immediately began to eat as fast as I could. I thought about saving some for Blade but didn't, it was all so good.

While I ate, my April scratched my ears and petted me softly. Did I die and go to heaven dear Universe? Is this what it's like up there?

If it is I accept this new life with much love. After all the bad stuff, to have my April and Maha love me so much felt like redemption. Did I do it all correctly dear Universe? I don't want to mess it up.

My April took the empty plate back down the stairway. I hesitated for a moment, which made her say….. "Hey! Come on down! Come with me little man!"

I never ran down a stairway so fast. I think I slid most of the way.

Wow! My house! My home! My April! Mine! Mine! Mine!

I scurried across the floor full of excitement at my new digs. The sun was out. The people box was on telling human stories. I remembered TV from Maha's house. There I had to share with Shannon and Tory. Now there was no need for sharing! It was all mine.

Pawprints To The Universe

I started to run around like a maniac. My April giggled at my antics. Boy this was turning out better than I ever could have imagined. It was all a special dream made just for me.

It was then as I ran through the kitchen I came face to face with a cat.

A cat!! No one had said anything about a cat. This one had big blue eyes. That was weird because most of the cats I had ever met had green ones. This one must be a mutant (I heard about mutants from a rat intruder that used to invade my under the porch space so long ago).

"Oh God! Another stupid dog." It leaned into me almost butting up against my snout. I had grown up not trusting cats. Most of them were sneaky and greedy. Not as bad as most humans like the mother said, but bad enough.

"So you are the long awaited puppy savior!" he hissed.

"You don't look so special. Just so we are clear, here are the house rules", he continued.

House rules! This is my house you stupid cat! Get out of my way.

Why didn't anyone tell me about this cat?

"Here are the rules according to me. I am Eros the Cat, beloved pussy cat of the April. What I say goes. You will not do the following". With that Eros began the list. A long list it was.

"Number 1". I have my own food and bowls! You are not allowed to even look at them. I have a special kitty diet that keeps me as gorgeous as I am!

Number 2. You are not allowed to go anywhere near my window bed. It's positioned perfectly for morning sun. I don't want your smelly butt stinking it all up.

Number 3. You are not allowed to bark at me for any reason. It upsets my delicate mental balance.

Number 4. If you urinate or poop in my litter box, you will die a painful slow death.

Number 5. All treats are intended for me. I am the prince of this house, so that makes everything mine!

Number 6. If you poop in the house and then you try to pin it on me we will come after you with a vengeance.

Number 7. The lap of the April is mine..... Not yours."

Boy what a pushy cat! I listened like I understood and would comply. However, I was already searching for the opportunity to tell this furry lump off. Put the stupid thing in its place as soon as I could.

My April came over to sit with me on the couch. She smelled so good. Her fingers played with my floppy ears. It was all so perfect. The hum of the house was peaceful. There were other cats as well. One guy named Tempest was friendly. He came over and introduced himself. He said there were other dogs here, but I had not seen one. Did she keep them locked up somewhere? I hope not, but then again so far I felt like the King of the house. I just hoped she would let me out to pee soon. As I sat on the couch my tummy began to rumble. Oh great. Now I had to poop. What should I do? Dear Universe, please guide me. Should I tell her? Would she be mad? Would I get in trouble? I didn't know. So I sat there trying not to poop, which was pretty impossible. I had had an abnormally big breakfast, so of course poop would be the next event.

I watched my April in the kitchen. She kept smiling at me. I was so nervous because I knew soon I would poop on the couch. My April would send me back to the mean one and all would be lost.

Frantically I wiggled around hoping the worst would not happen, yet it was.

Oh no!

Here it comes.

Just at that moment my April put down her towel and said "Sweetie! Are you okay?" Oh no! She was gonna know pretty quickly that I was a messy puppy. I tried to stop it but all at once it just came out. I buried my head into the couch waiting for the first blow.

"Oh Guinness! Honey! Are you okay? Oh boy, it smells like poop. Did you have an accident? Oh it's all my fault! I should have let you out first thing".

I couldn't' believe my ears?! She wasn't mad! OMG! She wasn't mad!

I cried a little to show I was sorry but she took all the blame.

"Come on, lets get you cleaned up." With that she scooped me up in her arms. She ran some warm water in the sink and gave me a good bath. It felt so good to have her rub my body. The warm water calmed me down. In the end she wrapped me in a fluffy towel. It ws so cool!

After we finished she let me outside. I shook off all the excess water while taking in the warm sunlight.

She wasn't mad!

She probably hadn't seen the couch yet. Punishment could still happen.

"Let's clean this up", she said with a smile.

I had never been so lucky. Instead of being evicted, I was sitting with her while she cleaned up my poop. Wow, so weird. I truly have come to heaven.

Thank you dear Universe. I wouldn't be here if you had not loved me. No one else did…. Wow so cool!

79

A Cat Called Eros

Dear Universe,

My life has changed so much. Everyday there is new stuff. Stuff that was confusing for so long for a puppy like me. Every day is fun. The only problem so far is this uppity cat called Eros. He's claiming that my April is his April and that I am an imposter.

I am not!

Stupid cat never had a rough day in his life. Always had the April to look out for him. Never had the problems I have had trying to find her. He says I'll never be cool enough for him. I've spent quite a bit of time yelling at him for being so stupid. If I had barked this much when I was with the mean one she would have been so mad. My April never yells or gets mad. Sometimes I know I am a pain in the butt. Sometimes I don't understand what the right thing to do is. That's why it's so cool for you dear Universe to be my friend. I bet you never heard of the cat called Eros. He claims to be so "in tune" with you the Universe, but I know that he's not. For crying out <u>loud</u> dear Universe, he's a cat! How connected could he really be? Ok, Ok, I know….. be nice. Well I try to be nice but Eros always acts all superior. He's <u>not</u>! It's hard to be nice when he acts snarky. I guess I will become less irritated as time goes on but it's hard with him right now.

The best part of any day is bedtime. My April fluffs up the pillows with all the warm blankies. I can hardly wait to dive in every night. I get as close as I can every time. She always holds me close to her. So much hugging I can hardly stand all the joy. Of course Eros stakes his claim on the pillows above her head. He often glares at me as I nestle down under the covers. He makes sure he purrs real loud. Not sure what his point is. I am so happy that absolutely nothing can damper my spirits!

80

This Place Called Los Angeles

Dear Universe,

Today I went to the park with my April. It was different then the parks with Maha. It was winter where she is. It would snow, rain, and sleet a lot. Often it was really cold. Here in this place called Los Angeles it was like summertime. I felt giddy with happiness. The green trees colorful flowers and sunshine made me feel so good. In the park it was always me and my April. We would see the same people over and over. Soon they knew our names. They would say "hi" and scratch my ears. There were firemen who came to the park for exercise. There was one of them that would yell "GUINNESS!" when he walked into the park. Everyone knew who I was. It was so odd to be the center of attention.

Pawprints To The Universe

I would have to get on my tippy toes to say hi to everyone. I often wonder how I went from starving puppy to popular puppy. Was it my plan dear Universe? I never thought much about spiritual stuff. I guess I was so focused on survival, I missed some opportunities. Maybe it's not every day but I do think about a lot of things. Maybe it's called giving up. Maybe it was all the bad stuff. All I do know is that you have always been my friend dear Universe. Even when I was under the porch with my brother. The mother always told me stories about you. She said I could trust you and she was right.

Every day I feel loved.

Everyday I know more about who I am as a puppy. My April looks out for me. Everyone in this planet has some good in them, don't they. Well maybe not the mean one, but most of the others are really cool.

81

Our Walk

Dear Universe,

Today when we went for our walk I saw another puppy that looked so much like my brother Blade. At first I was certain it was him. I even pulled on my leash to get a better look. My April was surprised I was being so aggressive because I usually was more relaxed. This, however, was an exception. If it was him I wanted to tell him about my good fortune. All the wonderful things that happened since we last saw each other. Blade had a bad cough at the time. I wondered if he still had it.

Fortunately my April let me run over to this dog who looked so much like him. Sadly, once I got closer I could see it wasn't him. This dog said he was George. He was kind of silly in the fact that he acted like a mean dog. I could see in his eyes that he was unhappy. His human jerked him away from me. His eyes looked woeful.

"My dog is vicious", said the human.

"Oh, okay", said my April.

I knew that wasn't true. He was being abused. I looked up at my April hoping she would do something. When we came to a picnic table in the park she sat down and pulled me onto her lap.

"Oh Guinness! I know you are sad about that poor puppy. We can't unfortunately save everyone."

"Why?" I asked. "I got saved."

"Well, that's because you met me. Not everyone would find you and take you 3000 miles back with her. You are a lucky puppy! You should thank the universe every day!"

I knew that. Obviously she did not ever find my letters to you dear Universe. I think she would be proud of me if she knew.

Pawprints To The Universe

We sat on the picnic table for quite a while. I jumped down to look at a bug crawling under the table. All of a sudden I was back under the porch with Blade. He was crying that he was hungry. It had been a rainy day so I could not go out to see if anyone had dropped any crumbs. There was a huge bug that scurried by. I pounced on it immediately. My belly was growling with hunger too. Blade needed it more that I. So I dragged it over to him. At first he was scared of the wiggly legs. My paw stopped the movement. Blade leaned forward scooping the bug up quickly. I was pleased that he at least had the bug in his belly. I remember crying as well. It was so miserable, yet comfy under that porch. It was the warmth of Blade's belly that made it comfy.

Being under this picnic table reminded me of the fears of that experience. I also know that that was when I started talking to you dear Universe. The mother always told me you would answer. It was a gift that mother gave me as it has kept me strong all this time.

Under the picnic table today it all came back to me with great sadness. I started to shake uncontrollably. My April who had been enjoying the trees bent down under the table and crawled under it with me.

What was she doing?

Her arms wrapped around me. She was concerned with my trembling. In her arms she rocked me while whispering everything was okay. I knew it was, but the image of Blade made me sad and scared that maybe he didn't make it.

He said he would never leave like the mother, but somehow at the so-called shelter he disappeared. Never to be seen again. I never asked it before but is Blade up there with you dear Universe? It would give me comfort to know that you were looking after him. Could you check to see if he's there for me?

My April and I stayed under the picnic table for a long time. My body continued to tremble, but the warmth of being so close to someone who loves me helped to calm me down.

"If I didn't know better Guinness, I'd say you have PTSD", said my April.

"Oh, it's past events that return to your awareness to haunt and scare you. Something bad must have happened to cause it."

My April blamed the mean one. Yes that contributed as well. The truth was under that old porch when there was little hope of a morsel of food when you were starving. It was watching your beloved brother slowly get weaker. Yes, dear Universe, it was a terrible experience. You were right though. It did pass and we were found. Though I suspect that it was too late for Blade. Please let me know where he is if you can do that. I truly hope he is with you. If he's still here than I would wish to find him and bring him here with me. It would make me happy to share my good fortune It would be with reluctance that I would share my April. She belongs to me..... she really does.

82

Too Good To Be True

Dear Universe,

My new life is full of surprises. We settled into a routine kinda like when I was at Maha's. The only bad thing about Maha's was that the mean one could still lay claim to me. I heard she came up to look for me when I allegedly ran away. She didn't feel it was urgent enough to come find me for a couple of weeks. I guess she didn't think I really ran away.

Why? Why dear Universe is she so mean and disconnected? The mother used to tell me that all humans were bad. I can remember watching them finding that indeed the mother was absolutely right. Most of them are mean. Maha and my April were the best humans I ever met. Why did it take so long for me to find them? I know you told me that it was important to have all the experiences I could….. good and bad. Ok I did, but why did it take so long?

And don't tell me I made all the choices. Why would I choose to be born under an old porch with little food and hardly no love? The mother was warm and loving but why didn't she come back? Maybe Blade could have felt better. I did everything I could to help him. He needed the mother's loving embrace to live well and healthy. I wish I could see what happened with him. I check the park every day with my April. Everyone knows me there. I have become quite popular. No one though has any idea where Blade might be. Of All the other puppies I have asked, simply not one of them had any clue. I hope he's okay. It would be so cool to have him here with me in my new digs. We could run in the park together every day with a big plate of food when we finished. It would be so perfect.

Each day I look for him. Maybe some day I will get lucky. Dear Universe, if he ever shows up where you are please tell him I am looking for him. He would complete part of my journey. So let me know if he does. Maybe you could arrange for him to show up. I heard that the Universe always listens and provides. This is the only request left on my list. I'll understand if you can't do it but I thought I'd at least ask.

So every night I snuggle up under the covers. Every night my ears are rubbed to perfection. The soft blanket wraps me up in all the love I can create. In the morning I lick my April's nose and she giggles while hugging me close. Oh that's another new thing. My April always calls me over by saying "Guinness come get close!" Of course I want that but was never encouraged to get too close. When I did there was usually trouble, especially with the mean one. I have to admit at first I was reluctant to get too close. My April though was very persistent in her requests. Finally I just gave in while snuggling close. It was all too good to be true.

83

Am I An Old Soul?

Dear Universe,

I should also talk about my new roommates. It seems that my April had four other dogs before me. There was a Chow named Ra that everyone said was an old soul. Old soul, what the heck does that mean? Yes. Yes. I know what a soul is. Everyone has one. You told me that yourself dear Universe. The problem I have is that what makes a soul old? You said yourself that the days were not meant to be numbered. If that is true, why is there new, old, and in-between? It's so, so confusing for me. I wish I was smarter about the ways of the world. That's why I have you dear Universe. Guide me and teach me how to be a better puppy.

So am I an old soul? How do I find out what other times we have been together as puppy and human? I know you told me that we have been here

Pawprints To The Universe

a lot of times. I know that my April was who I was looking for, for so long. Now that we have been reunited I want to know. Please tell me dear Universe. Maybe when I snuggle in bed tonite I will dream about it. Maybe I could even find Blade if I am lucky.

Okay, so is it a deal? Let me know as soon as you can. I want to be the best puppy every in this life. Now that I am home I can start doing good things with my new situation.

When nighttime comes I await the beauty of sleep. I can see the dream unfolding.

Good night dear Universe.

84

Now I Understand

Dear Universe,

Okay. I think I understand now. Thank you for dreaming with me last night. The story of me was a good one. Apparently I have had quite a few experiences. In some of them I was brave and others fell short in the warm and fuzzy department. All in all, it's a bit overwhelming because I thought I was just a puppy who had rotten luck. Thank goodness the mother told me about you. She said that the universe is my friend. Every time I came into a body you would be there to help and guide me. Last night you showed me all that. It was so cool!

Now I understand why it was so important for me to find my April. It was not just finding my own human. It was to find her! We had been together many times. We always were loving and kind with each other. Now we were getting another change to be together. After all the struggle, now we could stay together in this life for a long time.

I felt very possessive of her. I found that just the mere thought of her and any other puppy was just too much for me to bear. I had found her and she was not getting away.

Yes. Yes. I know we all have this free-will thing. So tell me dear Universe, how could I choose to not meet up with my April first thing when I got here? So much suffering. I know things worked out for me but what about the mother and Blade? Neither of them were ever seen again. Please let me know if they are there with you. I want to know, yet I do not want to know. The wish that they can still be here with me fills my heart up every day. So please dear Universe, let me know.

The mother left us under the porch to fend for ourselves That was so confusing because I could feel that she loved us both.

Blade, with his soft paws and wet nose, always would snuggle close especially when it rained.

85

Tata

Dear Universe,

I have spent a lot of time exclaiming over my good luck at finding my forever home. There are other critters here in this house as well. It's most likely going to be a challenge to keep them from my April. There are two chow chows and a whole bunch of cats. Why she would have cats is beyond me. As soon as I arrived a few of them tried to smell my butt. What made them the bosses? Nothing does. I know that. They think they are before me with the April. It is my mission to make her all my own.

The two chows were a different story. There was Tata, and Anubis. They were adopted just like me. They did not however come from far far away. None of them had ever been on a big truck. They did not even know what snow was. They claimed that there had never been any snow here ever. That's weird!

Tata was the leader. She reminded me a lot of Tory. All full of advice for a puppy like me. She said that it was okay with her if I stayed. My naturally snarky mouth almost got me into trouble. I reminded her that my April went to a lot of trouble to get me here. Her approval or disapproval made no difference to anyone. Well, that did not go over very well. Tata was a big doggie, almost 100 lbs. she constantly bragged. She said she could eat me up and spit me out if I didn't shut up. Well I didn't.....

Tata had a scary voice. She vowed to bite me (well that would mean she would have to catch me). Since she was so big it was easy to escape her clutches. We spun around the living room. I ran up the stairs swiftly jumping through the steps to safety when she almost got me. It was actually a lot of fun. Tata wasn't having fun, but I sure was!

I guess we made a lot of noise because my April came in from the kitchen wanting to know what was going on! Tata almost ran into her. We both skidded to a stop. My April stood there with her hands on her hips. She looked mad. Oh no! I hope I didn't screw this opportunity up with my shenanigans. I was prepared to blame it all on Tata and maybe even Anubis. I was scared though that I might get sent back to the abandoned porch for misbehavior. Just the thought of it made me start shaking. I couldn't stop.

My April reached down and picked me up. Oh man! I had my sorry speech all prepared. I could not for the life of me stop shaking.

"Oh Guinness!" she whispered in my ear.

"You need to be a nice boy. Tata has been here a long time. She has had some bad times just like you."

Oh boy gosh! I did not know. Tata had lived under a car in downtown Los Angeles. Someone had covered her in motor oil and left her to die. Just like me she had been left behind. My April wanted me to be nicer so I said ok. She put me back down on the floor as I moved towards Tata. Maybe I should give her a sloppy kiss to make up.

I leaned forward to be nice and Tata lunged towards me and bit me in the ribs. Ouch!!! Of course I could not let that insult pass, So as she retreated up the stairs I called her a big fat butt! I know I should have kept my snout closed but she really cheesed me off.

"I don't have a big butt!" she screamed!

"Yes you do!" I screamed back. My April scooped me up. If ever I was going to get in trouble it would be right now! My April took me outside for a "time out". What was that? Was I gonna get a spanking or yelled at? I didn't know.

We sat on the porch steps while the April told me that living here with her would require my being nicer to everyone. I did not have to fight anymore. I thought the slap would be next, but it wasn't.

"Come get close", she whispered. Snuggled in her arms I was so happy. Not hits. No screaming….. No name calling. Just a request for better behavior.

Okay.

We stayed outside for a long time. I could see Tata looking at us from inside the living room. She was growling at me. I guess according to my April her feelings were hurt. I tried to explain that I was just calling it as I see it. Her butt was and is enormous, but okay I will apologize.

My April held me as we made our way inside. I manage to say "Sorry". Tata sniffed at me and said "Okay, you are forgiven.".

I couldn't help myself. I told her again how fat she was. So I guess Tata and I will remain distant until she gets over herself. My April asked me to be nice. I guess it's the least I can do.

Glancing across the room I saw Anubis. He also had a sad story, but he managed to land here at this house. He stared at me with a stupid grin on his face. He also had been abused, or so he said. He said he was almost executed a while back. He said he was saved by my April just in the nick of time. He said he had committed his life to protect her from evil. It was something he was committed to. Apparently he had a better sense of humor than Tata because he was cracking up over my fat butt statement. I liked him immediately.

I knew that I had to watch my behavior. Having been a scrapper, I now had to be nice. Oh boy. I just hope I can pull it off.

86

Eros

Dear Universe,

I am so glad you are proud of me! It's really hard to be nice. Sometimes I mess up but I never really get in trouble. Our little talks with my April help me to be a better puppy. Tata and Anubis at the end of the day are puppies too. So we have a better chance to get along.

I now need to talk about the cats. My god! There are so many of them. They are all self-entitled nightmares. They eat and sleep all day long. They poop in weird boxes that are stinky. They claim they keep the house free of mice, but I still see mice sometimes. They are slackers. There needs too be absolutely no mice running around here. They used to be a tasty morsel back in the day. Now, not so much. It started to annoy me that the cats thought they were so superior. I guess they thought that since there was so many of them.

Apparently there was a ring leader called Eros. Oddly the name means love. He might act all lovey-dovey, but he's a meanie. Right from the start he was all up in my face. Saying that the April belonged to him. He was the only pet in the house that mattered. There were about 10 cats in total plus the 2 chows, so the best I could hope for was being number 13 on the list.

I was furious. Who did this hot shot pussy cat think he was? He claimed he was the love of her life, not me!! Strutting his stuff upstairs like he owned the place. My question was why was he sequestered upstairs. He said he was such a high class pussy cat that he could only be in high places.

Really?

Eros was so full of himself. He never had known a hungry day. He was never abandoned. He never was starving. He never had anyone hit him on the snout. His inability to understand my plight made me so mad!

He never missed a chance to sneer at me. To him I was a low class puppy from parts unknown. Mostly I stayed downstairs, only going upstairs when it was time to sleep. It was tricky to get up there without running into Eros. My April said it was a big bed and that there was room for both of us.

So we would settle in each night on either side of her. We glared at each other while snuggling in close. He on her right. Me on her left.

It should have been okay but Eros said I stunk like a dog and that it made him sick to his stomach. HE demanded my removal. Of course the April tried to mediate, but cat smell can be, and in this situation is, just as stinky or worse.

My April begged both of us to make up. We both nodded our head, but did nothing to make a positive connection.

Apparently it was going to be war. Since I had a loud bark I was always the one who looked guilty. Eros took full advantage of that! I struggled to be good but he whipped me up into a frenzy every day. The little jerk knew what he was doing.

The only saving grace was the fact my April loved me. She never raised her voice or hand to me. She had the ability to calm me down with just her words. I tried to talk her into getting rid of Eros. I know he was doing the exact same thing in her other ear. This went on for quite a while. My April was very skilled at keeping us apart. The only dangerous ground was at night when we were supposed to be sleeping. I tell ya I slept with one eye open with that crafty cat sleeping on the other side of the woman I loved.

Everyday we managed to fight over my April. He just did not understand that she was mine, all mine! How hard was that to understand? I don't care what stupid pedigree he might have. He said I was a mutt, a Heinz 57, a scatter brain dog. It's all I was according to him.

So the fight continued.

For the sake of my April I tried to be a good boy. It was so hard when he teased me.

Sometimes in those times I wanted to make him shut up but he was always just out of reach.

87

The Pool

Dear Universe,

California is a cool place. The other pets in this house tell me they don't even know what snow is. I was very surprised while not being quite sure how that could be.

I did not know too many cats before I came here. In the early days they were often quite helpful finding rats and bugs to eat. I guess you would call them feral cats as they had no caretaker either. So what does that make me?

At Maha's house the only cats I saw were outside. Often on our walks around the point we would see an occasional cat. I can remember wanting so bad to chase them. Tory told me that that was a stupid thing to do, as I would never ever be able to catch them. Regardless, I still wanted to chase them. Here, most of the cats are inside only. It makes them so much easier to chase!

Adjusting to what the rules were was hard. My April loved all of us but of course she loved me most. She only asked me to be nice so the house would be in harmony.

Now, I really agreed to the terms hoping there would be a few loopholes. I had to make sure though that I tried my best. So far I have not gotten yelled at. What's cool is that I was told there was no yelling in this place. The chows said they ever heard any mean stuff. They laughed because they said they did a lot of stuff they should not of. It was because they were pure bred that they could. I was told I was a mutt.

A mutt?

You know I may have had a slow start but I was starting to realize how cool I actually was. The chows were like a family of mean puppies. They said that they weren't worried about me cuz I probably would die in a tussle with them. They thought that sooner or later I would make a dumb move and it would be game over. (Whatever that means.)

The female chow named Tata was running the chow show. She said I was a pipsqueak who really did not deserve to be here. But she put up for me for my April's sake.

Really?

I argued back every day. Every day they told me my days were numbered. Oh no! Just when everything was working out I had to wrangle these big dogs.

Tata said I would probably fall in the water and drown.

Water?

What water?

There was an ocean where I came from. Probably more water that Tata could imagine. Obviously she did not know who she was dealing with.

Whatever.

I knew I was where I had always been destined to be. So dear Universe, how do I deal with these chows? I probably could take them on but if they all ambushed me at once it could be bad.

Ok!

You're saying I should just be me….. Guinness….. who by some miracle found the human I always knew existed. Be me? I guess I never have given it much thought.

Ok.

I will be me. Now that I am safe with no worries of survival maybe I can get in touch more with you dear Universe.

I just noticed that there is a pool of water outside. It's pretty small compared to the ocean, but for some reason there is one here.

The Allen took me out. I was trying to be independent so I stayed across the pond from him. He was supposed to be watching me but sometimes he would focus on other stuff. I took the opportunity to investigate.

"Guinness?"

"Guinness?"

"Where are you"?

Drat!

I popped my head up to let him know I was there.

"Good boy!"

Well of course I am good. My confidence is improving. In this new life I am a puppy of importance. I can do anything!

"Guinness! Come over here!"

There he goes again. I guess I should go over there. How to get there? I wasn't sure, then I just jumped in the water. It was like a short cut.

My legs began to do a walking motion. Wow! I was walking on water..... well maybe it was more *in* the water. Any, I was making my ways over to the Allen.

"Oh my god! Guinness?"

"You are swimming! I didn't know you could swim!"

There is lots about me you don't know! The Allen had just met me but we were still getting to know each other. Of course I had never had to swim before, but when I jumped in I just started to move my legs. It felt weird but I had my head above water. Slowly I crossed to the other side as the Allen clapped his hands. Yes! I am a good boy. I liked the idea that the Allen was surprised. He needed to know how talented I really was.

I reached the other side where he was sitting. The Allen sat there all proud of me.

Okay.

How do I get out now?

I bounced back and forth hoping I would get some help. I could hear Tata and Anubis laughing from the window.

Why were they laughing? Was it because I may potentially be trapped in the small lake?

Hey Allen!

Help a guy out!

Can you get me out?

The Allen stood up and came towards me. Oh good! I guess I won't drown He reached down pulling me up onto the cement.

"Didn't plan on how you were going to get out, did you?"

Ok Allen, you're right. I thought I could just climb out. Thanks buddy for pulling me out. I could have figured it out..... Really. I could have.

So now I was soaking wet. I shook off as much as I could. The chows were in the window laughing at me. Apparently they had not swam in the pool. I was a "natural"..... yes I was.

Tata said I was a puny excuse for a dog! The Anubis was a bit more kind. He understood that I had had a rough time. He didn't make fun of me. Tata, however, did all the time. I took it as long as I could..... then I yelled as loud as I could to you dear Universe. The announcement was that she had a HUGE fat butt. I was repeating something I said before but now the whole neighborhood could hear it.

Well fed.... Fat butt.

She of course got really mad. Today, however, she was locked up in the house and I was with the Allen.

Yeah! I was with the Allen. Right now he was rubbing my ears while praising my bravery. He obviously was a very smart human to notice all of my talents.

Before I came here I didn't know that talent existed. I think this is what you meant dear Universe about discovering my purpose and who I am.

The Allen told me to sit in the sun until my fur dried off. It felt so good to do that. Me and the Allen….. two guys….. enjoying the day.

I'm sorry I didn't believe you dear Universe when you told me I would be happy someday. At the time everything was so hard. I was so hungry. Blade and the mother would have loved this. Maybe some day they will find a good home like me. I know they are with you but maybe someday they will come back. That would be so cool.

Anyways. I spent the afternoon in the sun….. way better than under a porch in relentless rain.

88

A Birthday, or Christmas?

Dear Universe,

I am settling in very well. I had my first holiday, which I never knew existed! It's a human day celebrating someone's birthday. Gosh, I don't even know if I ever had a birthday. My April says she thinks it's in the summer, like July or August. I don't know for sure but this particular birthday iis pretty special. Why? I don't know.

My April said we were going to the Allen's mother's house. He said he had a couple of brothers and a sister. We were going to his mother's house, and that I had to be a good boy.

So we boarded the car. It was a long drive, but I was tucked in my April's lap. A few times I jumped over to the Allen so he would not feel left out. It was pretty cool that I had two laps to choose from.

It was a really long drive. Falling asleep seemed to be the only way to handle it.

When we got there my April carried me in. Everyone came over to pet me. That was pretty cool. Then mother of the Allen was in the kitchen. She was stirring a big pot of something. I did not want to get in trouble but I was really hungry. Being so small I wasn't able to see what was up on the counter.

"Don't give Guinness any food!" yelled my April from the other room.

"Okay. I won't", replied the mother of Allen.

My face must have shown my disappointment. Whatever she was doing, it smelled good. I stayed in the kitchen for awhile. I learned at Maha's that once in a while food found its way to the floor. Maybe that would be the case today. Making myself comfortable, I caught her eye. She smiled at me as she picked up something small and round. It had a little smoke rising up from it. My mouth just wanted to bite it and eat it all up. It was handed to me gently.

"Here you go Mr. G. It will be our little secret", she said.

Secret?

Could I trust her?

The mean one had little secrets that never worked out for me. Somehow I was blamed and punished, all for a little secret. So I had to be really careful. She put it close to me. What should I do? I wanted to snatch it out of her hands, but she was so nice to me that I really wanted to be nice. I gently took the small ball from her hand. Immediately the taste filled my mouth. Oh my god! So so so good!

Was there more?

I lost all sense of reason hoping against hope there would be one more piece.

There was!

Oh my God!

It melted in my mouth!

The mother of the Allen told me to keep quiet. It was a little secret I could live with. Apparently not all secrets are bad. She then shooed me back into the living room.

They were all sitting around tearing paper off of boxes. Pretty weird. All of them were smiling and laughing. Of course I plopped myself on the floor in the middle of all the action. So this was Christmas. I didn't know what that meant, but I did like all the good energy. At first I was afraid to move. What if I did something stupid? What if I had to pee and they didn't let me out? So many "what ifs" made me very nervous.

My April sat next to me. Her hand rubbed my back. I was having a hard time keeping my eyes open. There was an Aunt Dee that sat on the other side of me. All of a sudden she stood up and asked me if I needed to go outside.

Really?

How did she know dear Universe that I did have to pee? No one had ever asked me before, so I was really surprised and happy. I didn't even have to

Pawprints To The Universe

wear a leash….. she just opened the door and out I went.

I think I sprinkled a lot of pee everywhere in that yard. There was a breeze after I looked out over the hill. It was beautiful The Aunt Dee and my April let me run until I dropped. The Allen came out too, with a ball in his hand. What the heck was that for? He called my name and threw it. All of a sudden I just had to get that ball. The Allen must need it for something. It was cool to run back to him with it in my mouth.

Then…..

He threw it again!

Again!?

What was up with him? He lost his ball, I went and got it. I ran it back to him. Why was he throwing it again?

Humans.

Pawprints To The Universe

Dear Universe, what is up with them? Sometimes they do strange things. Not that I was complaining. It was huge fun running to get the ball. If this is what he felt he needed to do, I was glad to go get it for him.

We played ball for quite a while. I still don't understand why, but the Allen always seemed happy when he threw it. It felt wonderful to be around laughter.

I was getting so tired though. Just when I felt I couldn't do it one more time, the mother of the Allen brought out a huge bowl of water.

For me?

Wow.

It is all for me. I drank it so fast I choked a little. Looking up at all of them, I felt so loved and cared for. So this is what it is like to have a family.

Cool.

The sun was starting to go down. Everyone was back in the living room. There was ribbon and paper all over the floor. It was so fun to run into the pile. It went everywhere. No one seemed to mind. I forgot to worry about being in trouble.

Is this how it is dear Universe? A family to love you, fresh water, good food? And most importantly, getting to pee and poop without getting yelled at?

It's like a beautiful dream. I bit a ribbon and destroyed it. For a moment I was scared. Didn't have to be though. My April was not mad. She just worried it might give me a tummy ache.

It didn't.

We ate these little balls of meat for dinner. The mother of the Allen had cooked them.

I was getting human food again?

Wow.

Christmas is a great day. I fell asleep on my blanket on the couch. I was on the couch and no one got mad.

So cool.

When we left to go home the Allen held me on his lap as my April drove the car. I fell asleep and slept all the way home.

Yes home.

I had a forever home.

How cool is that?

Thank you dear Universe.

89

The Guinea Pigs

Dear Universe,

Help! I am being overtaken by weird little creatures. My new home is filled with them. I have tried to behave but these little things are making it virtually impossible.

I have been here with my April for a few weeks. We made it through Christmas and have moved on to the full experience in this place called California.

I have come to the conclusion that there are just too many animals here. There are at least 10 cats, 3 dogs (includes me), goats, weird things with shells on their backs, and a whole bunch of birds. It's pretty packed here.

There is a woman called the Diane who comes over often to clean up after all of us. She's cool cuz she thinks I'm pretty cute. She is a dog lover and huge animal person. I loved her from the start. She's the one who showed me the little fuzzy creatures. She called them pigs.

They lived in a small plastic pool. They ran around so fast that I figured they should be more organized. I took on the role of dictator as I tried to get them where they should be.

I jumped into the container and began training them to be obedient pigs. It was actually a lot of fun disciplining them. The Diane and my April would laugh as I began the training. I did not intend to hurt them….. just discipline them so they would know who was boss.

Yes I am getting more confident. I just realized the other day that I am really in charge here. My April even calls me the "boss". She always laughs when I "boss" the pigs around. I was told to be nice at all times. Well dear Universe, that is quite impossible when they don't listen.

So yes dear Universe, I was a bit of a bad boy. These little things drove me crazy. I had to keep barking at them to settle them down..... Sheesh.....

The Diane would tell me to be kinder to the pigs. I tried. I really tried. My restraint leaving me defenseless every time.

So it went for a couple of months. The pigs finally moved out to be on their own (at least that is what my April said).

I could see them through the window (they were now on the porch). All of my lectures went right out of their little heads. I still give advice through that window. The Diane said they were worried I would mistakenly hurt them..... thus the move.

Really!

Never would I hurt them! They just needed direction. Please dear Universe, tell them I will still watch out for them.

Another weird thing was the discovery of the sticks. My April would give them in bunches to the pigs. At first I wasn't sure what they were. The pigs would get all excited when she put them in their habitat. They would all gather around eating them as fast as they could. So was it food? Hmmm…….

About a week later I was helping my April with what she called animal chores. She would bring food and water to all the critters, which I thought was cool. Imagine. A human remembering that all animals should eat well. So it was with great love that I helped everyday with the "animal chores".

I could see the bunch of sticks that went to the pigs. My April said they were called carrots. They had no smell. There were leafy things at the top. Why would the pigs get so excited about this dear Universe? It is a complete mystery to me.

90

Carrots

Dear Universe,

Today I encountered some weird stuff that my April was feeding to the guinea pigs.

Well the cat called Tempest gave me some advice. (He's really the only cool cat in the house.) He said I shouldn't judge what other critters eat until I tried it.

Why?

"Well if you want to become evolved, you have to consider other awarenesses", he replied.

Wow. That is a lot of big words. Why can't I just say it looks stupid? There's no smell. It rolls around the floor and it's hard to bite into. (Yes I tried but couldn't get it to stop rolling.)

So dear Universe, "awareness" is important too. There are so many things I don't understand yet. You say these things are called what? Ah. Carrots.

Now that my belly is always full I can think about these things more. Tempest called me a coward because I did not taste it for myself. I was getting pretty annoyed with him. He just kept pushing me to try it.

"Why don't you eat it?" I exclaimed.

"I'm a cat, that's why."

So what difference did that make? I tell ya the more cats I meet the more it's obvious what jerks they are. They think they are better than anyone! Well I was just going to ignore him. What did he know anyway!

The next day I was helping my April when she dropped a carrot from the bundle she was carrying. I watched it roll behind the couch. Funny thing was that my April did not notice. It just laid there waiting for me to investigate.

My April was very focused upon feeding the pigs. Tempest sat on the back of the couch waiting for me to make a move.

So I did.

I walked right up to it. This time I got a grip. I casually walked into the kitchen. No one saw me but Tempest. He gave me two paws up for my bravery.

Is being brave part of being aware dear Universe?

I held the stick in my paws. All I had to do to prove my further courage was to take a bite. Just one bite….. then Tempest would forever have to shut up because I had been brave.

I knew it would be yucky food so I close my eyes and took a bite. As I chewed I realized it tasted really good. Not just really good, but magical. No wonder the pigs ate it so fast.

I slipped behind the door to finish my tasty morsel. I made sure to eat up all the crumbs so I wouldn't get in trouble.

Why did I not get carrots?

Was I stupid to eat them?

Well how could that be? They were so good. How would I get my April to let me have them?

Tempest the cat laughed at me. If he didn't have the guts to get off the counter to tell me to my face, then he was the coward. I barked at him to come down here so I could make him stop laughing.

I know dear Universe that being brave is important. That's why I am bravely telling Tempest that I could take him out. BUT! He wouldn't come down! He said I had a lot of evolving to do before he would do that.

Pompous cat!

The next day my April sat the carrots on the chair. While she was busy I managed to forage a few of them.

Slowly.

Very slowly.

Then I would dash into the other room to store them in my secret stash place.

I was obsessed.

The idea of having a stockpile of carrots made me feel secure. So my new mission was to steal/take as many as I could hide.

Things were looking up!

91

My Eye

Dear Universe,

Every Wednesday a woman named Diane came to clean the house. I'm sure it was mostly because of the cats. As I said before, they have these stinky boxes that they poop in. I always pooped outside. I did not make a smelly mess. Eros in all his glory was the guy who made all the messes.

So on Wednesday my job was to supervise the Diane as she cleaned. It was an important job that I took very seriously. I have become an important guy. My April always told me I was in charge of everything. What I thought and said mattered a lot. It was so different from the early days when I was a puppy and powerless.

So it was that I was supervising Diane upstairs that Eros and I had a showdown. As usual he was bragging about how he ran the house. He screamed over the vacuum cleaner that I was just a stupid dog. He said I should go back under the porch where I came from.

He just made me so mad! I chased him around the bed nearly missing his tail. The Diane told me to settle down but by then I was out of control. We dashed around until I cornered the jerk in a back room. He was up on a box above me.

Now I had him.

I told him how stupid an insignificant cat really was. I made sure to get right in his face so he would understand my message. I could see his face get all snarky as I continued. In an instant he wielded his paw over his head and hit me square in the face. I couldn't believe his gall. I am the one in charge….. my April said so.

Boom! OMG! HE hit me in the eye! Ow!! For a second it hurt then something warm started dripping down my face. Eros stood there with his paw in the air looking all smug. "Hey stupid! It didn't hurt. Is that all you got?"

Eros stared a me with wide eyes. Why was he doing that? Was he trying to psyche me out or something?

I kept telling him off but my eye felt funny. The Diane came into the room worried that I had gotten myself hurt.

"No! I am fine!"

Being more focused on the dumb cat, I didn't notice right away that I was bleeding.

Oh great! Just what I did not need. The Diane knelt down looking at the eye that hurt.

"Oh baby! I think you are hurt. Let's go see your mom."

I followed her down the stairway as she went to find the April. My left eye felt funny. There was gooey stuff on my snout and whiskers. What was going on? My April picked me up for a better look. It made my head hurt and for a moment I felt dizzy.

"Oh my God!" the April was upset. She immediately got my leash and announce we were going to the doctor.

The doctor!?? Oh no! I'm okay. Just gooey. Although I did have to admit my vision was blurry,. All the way there my April held me.

"It's gonna be okay baby", she whispered. It surprised me that I wasn't in trouble. I had been hit for far less. Okay. I admit I was very snarky with Eros, but I didn't want to be hurt. My eye was becoming more and more painful. I decided to curl up in my April's lap all the way there.

When we arrived she carried me in. I was glad because by then I felt terrible. She held me close which gave me a lot of comfort. The doctor took us right away because it looked pretty bad, so they said.

His name was Dr. Ancu. He was a nice man. He gently took me from the April and said he needed to look closely at my eye. By this time it hurt so bad I couldn't cooperate. A huge light shining in that eye as he delivered that bad news.

92

The Specialist

Dear Universe,

Well my eye was pretty messed up. I should have not chased after Eros into that small space. I should have listened to the Diane when she told me to stop yelling at him.

Shoulda', shoulda', shoulda'.

So there I was, sitting in a small room in my April's lap. Not sure if my shaking was from being scared or that it was from it was a cold room. Either way the news wasn't good.

The doctor went on to explain that part of my iris had been pulled out and was bleeding. It would need surgery.

No! No! No!

I mentally pleaded with my April to tell him NO! as well. Maybe if I went home to bed it would be all better in the morning. Right?

My April was crying but she was also speaking up for me. She told the vet that she was determined to keep my eye in place.

This vet was kind while he said the only thing that he could do was to take the eye completely OUT!! Oh no!

He said that I would need to go to an eye specialist. There was one in Pasadena just minutes away. He said that vet would be the one to save my eye.

I felt my April decide to be strong. She stopped crying, telling the doctor that indeed she would take me there the next day. She insisted on something to make my eye stop hurting. It was so cool that she knew it hurt so much. There was a young girl who said she was gonna take me in the back room. To give me a pain shot. As she slipped arms around me it suddenly occurred to me that I remembered Blade being taken into a back room. I never saw him again. The back room was a bad place. This I knew as truth. What if my April was being tricked? What if they just threw me away somewhere? If my eye didn't hurt so bad I would have fought more. Just when everything was working out, I was now on my way to a most certain death!

With the last glimpse of my April, I prepared myself for the worst. The girl's voice was soft. That made me feel a little better. Maybe dying wasn't so bad. Maybe I would see you dear Universe. Will you meet me at the door to heaven? Or wherever it is you live? It's certain that I might be coming soon. My eye throbbed in pain as the girl wiped it off. There was this thing with a pointed end on it. What was that? My certain doom! I have to say dear Universe how unfair this is. Right when I was just getting comfortable, something happens that appears to end my bliss.

"Ok Guinness, I am going to give you something to make you feel better. Stay still so I can do it."

I felt defeat since I hurt so bad I could not fight. Everything that had brought me here went through my head like a flood. So much emotion I just started to cry out loud. Please make it stop hurting, but return me to my April. If I am gonna die I want to be in her arms. Nowhere else.

Ouch!

She poked me with this sharp thing. This must be what happened to Blade. They must have killed him just like the cats under the porch predicted so long ago. My eye felt like it was falling out of my head. At least take me back to my April. If I die, I want to be in her arms.

The room became a little blurry. My eye settled down. I was wrapped in a warm blanket as we returned to the exam room where my April awaited.

She jumped up as we came in. There was no better feeling than her wrapping her arms around me. I could hear the vet tell her I would sleep through the night. She could leave me there over night so I could be watched. She declared that she would take me home. I could hear her heart beating next to mine. Whatever happened would be okay. Snuggling next to her the bright lights of the vet office hurt both my eyes. Just wanted to go to sleep, which is exactly what I needed.

As the car started, the hum of the motor relaxed me even more. I sat in her lap as she drove the car. My eyes were heavy. Just so glad she decided to take me home. It was the first time I ever had a home of my very own. Maha had always told me a forever home was something attainable. Just never really believed her till now.

By the time we pulled into the driveway I was out cold. The whispers of love in my ear, she carried me into the house.

My house.

My home.

My human.

It was perfect.

We sat on the sofa while she held me. Would we have to go upstairs to where the Eros was? I hoped not.

We ended up on the sofa. The April let me lay on her chest as she stroked my ears. There was a patch on my eye, so seeing clearly was not an option.

"You have to lay still baby", she whispered. "Tomorrow we are going to get your eye fixed."

Eye? Oh yeah, my eye!

I was so befuddled from the pain shot it was hard to remember why my eye was covered.

Drifting off to sleep I could feel my April underneath me. It was perfect..... well except for my injury.

Right now I felt great. There was a small bowl of water next to the couch. I suddenly realized that I was so thirsty. Feeling woozy from the pain killers, I tried to move closer to the bowl. In the process my April opened her eyes.

"What's up little man?" she asked. For a second I was afraid to tell her. Maybe it wasn't even my water. It could belong to anyone.

"You thirsty?"

"Let me get it closer to you", she said. With that she leaned over, picking up the bowl and holding it in front of me.

For a moment it felt wrong. I kept waiting for the snout slap that always came from the mean one. This time someone was really concerned about my getting a drink. I felt like I had died and went to heaven.

I drank until I couldn't drink anymore. The bowl disappeared as I lay back down. So different from other times I my life. How I wish there had been someone to hold the water bowl for Blade. There were times when the only water to be had was from the rain. Certainly no one holding a water bowl for him. Things have changed a lot since then.

Now I have my own human who holds the water bowl as I get a drink. I wish Blade could see me now! If I wasn't so tired I would try to find him. Right now feels so good through, being in my

April's arms. My eye doesn't hurt at all! Can I take the bandage off?

"Hey little man! Leave the bandage alone. Your eye is in bad shape. Tomorrow we are going to a specialist who can fix it", she said.

"Why a specialist?", I asked.

"Because you're special my boy", she replied.

That was something I never considered dear Universe. Me? Special? It seemed like a great story but nowhere along the way did I feel special. When I was at Maha's I had the fist inkling that I might be. However, it wasn't until I arrived here that it started to be true.

Me….. special….. I like the way that sounds.

I snuggled into my April as close as I could get. Her arms were around me. There was no place I would rather be. Right here…..

I slept until the sun was peeking through the curtains. My eye was starting to hurt again. My

Pawprints To The Universe

April had made the appointment. She was worried that if I walked by myself to the car I would get dirt in my eye. So she decided to carry me. I have to admit it was pretty cool. I kept my bad eye closed but it was a comfort not to have to walk. She put me on a pillow in the front passenger seat. I felt like a king! My eye was throbbing and everything looked blurry when I tried to see through it. I hope they can fix it.

We arrived right on time, so my April said. The waiting room was filled with puppies with eye problems. There was one that growled at me but one look from my April shut him up. If I had felt better I would have told him off, but I was starting to feel sick in my belly. Please dear Universe, do not let me throw up.....

Thanks dear Universe, no puking. We were called into a small room while a beautiful young woman walked into the room. This was the specialist? Oh boy. It doesn't look like she's a specialist. I could feel my mom tense up. All I could do was hope it would be okay.

They put me on a table with a bright light. The doctor leaned in to take the bandage off.

Oh no! Don't touch my eye!

Don't do it! Don't do it!

I guess I looked pretty vicious as the doctor jumped back.

Good.

I need to set the boundaries now.

No! Do not touch my boo boo eye!

My April stood up next to me on the table.

"Hey little man! Calm down. We have to let the doctor look at your eye. It might hurt but it needs to be done."

I wasn't sure.

I felt such pain. No one told me they were gonna touch it. No way!! No way!!

Pawprints To The Universe

In a flash my April had me in a bear hug pinning me on the table. Oh my god! It hurt so much! The whole time she rubbed my back, whispering how much she loved me.

I didn't want to cooperate but somehow the examination was pulled off. The bright lights made my eye hurt even more. I was relieved when it was all over.

I could feel the tenseness in my April as she held me. The doctor wrote on her paper for quite a while. When she finally looked up I knew it was bad.

"Well, Guinness has had part of his iris pulled out. We can save the eye but the surgery is a little tricky. We need though to operate straight away", she said.

Oh no! Can my April come with me? I tried to make a break for it but my eye was so sore I couldn't pull it off. I needed to run and get away. What if they took my eye out after all?

There were many fears in my mind that came to the surface that day. The time came for them to prepare me for the surgery. I could tell my April did not want to give me to the nurse. I kept my eyes on hers as they took me away. I felt like I might never see her again.

"I'll be right here waiting for you my little man", she whispered.

"Ok I'll be right back", I replied. Then the door closed. I just hoped it would not remain closed for ever.

They gave me another shot of something which made me sleepy and took away the pain. There was a small man who patted my head while I fell asleep.

He said "Don't worry Guinness, it's all going to be okay. You will be as good as new."

Please dear Universe, make it all be true. I have now a big chance to be happy. I don't want to miss out. Take care of me.

93

I Was So Happy

Dear Universe,

It was so cool to sit and be with you during my surgery. I was scared but you came to help me let go. All of the people were nice to me. They gave me a shot (which I really hate) but it made me feel better. The next ting I knew I was with you.

You told me my eye would be okay. You told me also about the mother and Blade. I always wondered what happened to them. The big surprise was that you brought them with you! I was happy to see them but was also sad because they couldn't share in my life.

The first to show was the mother. She was so beautiful. Her fur was soft and she looked like she had eaten a few good meals. She nuzzled me while telling me that she intended to come back but had been hit by a truck as she tried to cross the street.

It made me so happy to know that I had always thought she just forgot about us! Now I know she wanted to but just couldn't.

Next to show up was Blade. He projected his energy into my heart. He thanked me for the bug dinners saying he felt so loved by me. I could feel my self wanting to pull him back into the world so he could be my brother again. He said that the cough finally took him out. He knew that I had been adopted and was happy for me.

My heart hurt a little. If only he could be with my April. He might have made it. The shelter tried to save him but he was too far gone.

I wish we could have stayed with you dear Universe, but the surgery was coming to a close and I had to wake up. The mother and Blade said they would watch over me. Both were pleased I had finally found my human. Both cried with joy that I was so loved.

The place changed back to the operating room. I felt groggy but the woman told me she had be able to fix my eye. Right then I didn't really care. The only thing I really needed was my April. They said as soon as I recovered she was coming to get me. Oh how blissful that thought is.

I was taken to a room where they put a plastic thing around my neck. It felt awful. I thought they were trying to choke me. Apparently I was not supposed to touch my eye.

Okay.

I promise to not scratch my eye. So take this stupid thing off of me.

Right NOW!

No one would listen to me. They just patted my head and said my April was coming to get me. Surely she would get them to take it off.

94

That Darn Collar

Dear Universe,

My April showed up with a lot of hugs for me. I didn't really understand what all the confusion was. My eye felt fine. It was this stupid thing around my neck. I could hardly hold my head up. Surely the doctor would take it off as soon as my April got there. It seemed like it took forever. What if she didn't come to get me? What if she decided she had enough puppies already?

The young nice man came and got me. He was carful not to move me quickly. All I really wanted to do was sleep but was excited to know I was going home.

The doctor said I had to take an antibiotic (whatever that is) pain medication and drops to heal my eye up faster. It sounded like an okay thing. I felt fine. Well maybe I was a little shaky walking. This collar needed to go but the doctor said my April had to do tough love. If I scratched the eye I could mess up the surgery.

If they were listening they would have heard my fervent promise to <u>NOT</u> scratch my eye. Why didn't they believe me? Now they had convinced my April it needed to stay on.

My April carried me to the car. She said I should prepare for some pain because the pain medication was going to wear off. I could not hear her because I was snuggled in her lap. The whole day had been really hard. I wondered if Eros got in trouble for hitting me in the eye. I would have to see how that turns out. Dear Universe this is too much! It was bad to have an eye boo boo but it was also cool to see how much love there was.

Finally after all these years I got to find out what really happened to the mother and Blade. Now I know neither of them wanted to leave and to know they would be waiting for me.

It healed up the hole in my heart. Now I have to deal with a hole in my eye. So far it hasn't been too bad.

We arrived home. The Allen scratched my head telling me that it would all be okay. They eye was all covered up and no one had taken off the collar.

The Allen told me to ask my April when I suggested he remove the collar. Didn't he know I had already asked her?

Well I fell asleep between them on the couch. It was a delicious sleep. I could hear the hum of the house and felt safe.

95

Couch Medicine

Dear Universe,

I awoke with a jolt. I was on a pillow sleeping next to my April. My eye was on fire. I needed someone to make it stop NOW! My belly ached in hunger. My head hurt. My eye was on fire! Why wasn't anyone stopping the pain?

I tried to stand up but my legs were shaky. I could see the water bowl in the distance. No need to wake anyone up. I would just jump down and get some.

Oh Man!

I fell flat on my face. What had happened to my legs? I couldn't see out of my eye! The collar left me off balance.

So thirsty but couldn't get there while all of this was happening. My April woke up to rescue me.

"Guinness! What are you doing?"

That was just it. I did not know what I was doing. Everything was weird.

"Take this stupid thing off!!!"

No one, not anyone was listening to me. Maybe I just needed to show them both that this thing needed to go.

"Here. Let me help you Guinness".

My April gently lifted me over to the water bowl. So thirsty. So thirsty.

KLUNK!

Every time I leaned into the bowl the edge of the collar klunked against the bowl. My tongue was not able to reach the water. This was horrible!

Pawprints To The Universe

After many attempts I complained loudly. I didn't want to cause trouble. It was this collar that was causing the trouble.

Take it off!!!!

My April lifted the water bowl into the collar area. At long last my dry parched tongue got some water. Please dear Universe step in here and help me. How am I supposed to survive without water? How am I going to eat? This stupid thing keeps hitting the bowl. I can't eat either. It was so frustrating!

Suddenly my April picked me up for a chat. She said it was time for my medication. She put something in a lump of cheese, offering it to me to eat.

Really?

It smells funny. Hiding it in a lump of cheese so stupid. It stinks. Can't you smell it? I admit I was hungry….. very hungry. If the cheese didn't smell funny I might have tried it. Even the Allen tried to get me to swallow it. So <u>NOT</u> happening.

My April and I sat on the couch for a while. Apparently she gave up on the cheese. She had returned with some dog food that she put on her fingers. It was kinda unfair cuz the smell of it overcame me. I couldn't help but gobble it off her fingers. There was a brief moment when I realized she had snuck that pill into the food. By this time I was so hungry I didn't care. My belly settled down.

My eye itched so bad!

It also hurt so much!

Someone needed to first take the collar off, then make it stop hurting. Isn't there a pill for that? It turned out to be a tiny pill. So I chomped it down. After a bit I felt no pain. Okay this recovery might not be so bad after all. I was ready for a nap hoping the April would be there with me. I was pleased to see her return. Instead of snuggling she put me on her lap with a white tube in one of her hands.

"Now Guinness, we have one more thing we have to do..... eye drops. Now before you get all snarky this is something we have to do."

She removed the bandage. The bright light made it feel so weird. I knew right away that there was no way I was gonna let her put those drops in my eye. NO WAY!

I mustered up the strength to jump off the couch. It was hard to distract my April from her mission. I agreed she could do it but she would have to catch me first!

With that I jumped down racing back and forth in the living room. As I predicted, my slippery puppy mojo worked very well. I hoped she would tire out and give up. I was getting pretty tired. Hopefully I could return soon to my cushy blankets. After all, I was injured. Everyone should be nice to me.

My April left the room. She returned with the Allen. This was such good news. He and I were buddies. Of course he was gonna talk some sense into her.

The collar needed to go along with any stupid ideas about eye drops. They could not be good.

The Allen sat on the couch inviting me to sit with him. Well maybe it was steak time. Maybe since I was the steak guy I would be sure to get some. So I jumped up next to him. No steak.

The Allen held my collar. What was he up to? I decided to let him know how vicious I could be. I survived under that porch for a reason. I gave him my scariest face and growl.

It worked!

He stopped holding me. My April who was sneaking up behind us dropped the white tube dropper.

Ha!

See. Don't mess with me!

They both left the room. Maybe they were gonna give up. I was starting to get mad. Here I was injured by a vicious cat from upstairs. Wounded, I survived the surgery. Now I was trying to just get some rest.

Pawprints To The Universe

The two humans were trying to put toxic stuff in my injured eye. Now they were conspiring against me!

96

The Big Gloves

Dear Universe,

The Allen returned with big things on his hands. He had also put on a thick shirt. It was a very suspicious move. My April was all smiles, rubbing my ears just the way I liked.

They both thought they could somehow fool me. Well no way! I could smell their betrayal a mile away.

When the Allen grabbed me I bit into those stupid gloves he was wearing. I did my best scary growl. He was smart cuz I had all my attention on biting his face off and did not see my April come around from behind. Before I could try to bit her she had put the drops in my eye.

Oww!!!

It burned really bad. Why would these two people want to do that to me? Had I not already had a lot of pain in my life!?

The Allen let me go but the damage was done. They had successfully put that stuff in my eye.

It still hurt.

I am pretty mad right now.

I heard them talking about how they had to do it every four hours for the next fourteen days. Um..... you are not.

It was sure to be a battle. I felt bad cause they were supposed to love me. Why did they want to do that? That mean doctor must have poisoned their minds.

My April came over to give me more food. I couldn't eat by myself. It was soothing though to eat off her fingers. After a few minutes I forgave her for everything. She held me close while whispering love bites in my ears. She said they had to give me the medicine. My eye was in pretty bad shape. It's all that stupid cat's fault. He's the one I needed to beat up. When I get better I am going to do just that.

Okay dear Universe, I won't but I really want to. You must have squealed to my April because she also said that she was gonna keep Eros and I separate for now. Him upstairs..... me downstairs.

Well okay, but I'm still mad at him.

The Allen also came to hold me. I could tell he felt bad cheesing me off with those big gloves. I knew the drops were for me own good. I even forgot about the whole thing. I guess they weren't so bad after all.

It was on its way to a peaceful time before bed. I could sense they were anxious. Why? It was almost time for bed. If they could just take this stupid collar off. Then suddenly there was the Allen with those big gloves again.

Really?

So before bed we had to do the drops all over again. It was not good. I do, however, have to give them credit. To get me to do something I don't want to do doesn't work out too often.

No way!

Let's see dear Universe, it's late and they said we have to do it again in a few hours!

I will wear them down. It hurts so much every time. I don't care if my eye doesn't heal. I don't care! It hurts too much.

I am beginning not to like this tough love thing. Obviously the human who invented it did not have a hurt eye. Right now I would like to just pull it out and throw it away.

Ok. Never mind. I do want my eye, but it's a big price to pay.

97

Every Four Hours

Dear Universe,

My life has become all about taking or not taking the eye drops. I admit I was not cooperative. I admit that I bit in the Allen's gloves with as much force as I could. It was hell!

Every four hours the Allen held onto me while my April snuck up on me to put the drops in my eye. It stung so bad! The fact it was every four hours around the clock made me very anxious.

It looked like it made them very tired too. I thought they would sleep the night through..... but no. A bell rang every four hours prompting them to get up to put the ouchy drops in my eye. I really wanted to bite them both in the butt. I gave that a lot of thought every time the Allen wrestled me to the ground. At first I was really mad. I think I hurt the

Pawprints To The Universe

Allen a few times. When I was all worked up I didn't care. I was willing to do anything to make them stop. After it was all over I began to feel bad for being so mean. Not sure if my eye is any better. It's a bit blurry. There is nothing I would rather do than just scratch it to death.

My April tells me it's healing, that's why it itches. The Allen calls me his brave boy. He claims that I have not hurt him, but I know that I am a handful. It just doesn't feel very fair dear Universe. I have arrived in my new world but now I have an injury to recover from. I know I should be happy that I am being taken care of so well. Maybe Blade would have lived if the Allen and my April found me under the porch. Maybe Maybe Maybe.

The two weeks dragged on. We settled into a rhythm of getting hand fed by my April. I tried running away from the Allen but he was too fast and always caught me. Of course I would turn vicious, but in the end I wanted to kiss both of them. I never thought anyone could love me this much.

We were scheduled to see the doctor on a Monday morning. It was just me and my April. She didn't talk the whole way there. I hoped she wasn't mad at me. She said she was just scared about my eye. All I wanted was to take this stupid collar off. Tough love is the one love I could have done without.

After the first week my eye did not hurt anymore. Even though the eye drops were still needed, I guess I was a little more cooperative. I still gave the Allen a hard time, all the while hoping we didn't have to do it anymore. I guess both my April and I were worried we would have to keep doing eye drops every four hours.

The collar was my worst enemy. It banged into everything all the time. I couldn't even get a drink of water by myself.

We pulled into the doctor's office. I decided I was gonna talk her into taking the collar off. My April carried me into the waiting room. There sure were a lot of puppies here. Just about all of them had a big collar on. Such torture. I would have kept my promise to not scratch my eye. No one believed me apparently and the collar stayed on.

Pawprints To The Universe

We walked into the examination room. I stayed on my April's lap. The table top was cold and uninviting. The doctor came in with a smile. She shined a light right in m eye while letting me stay in my April's lap. She said it was all healing nicely.

Okay. It's healing. Please tell me I can take the collar off. Ultimately she said two more weeks.

Oh no!

Not two more weeks!

I was so furious!

My April sighed and said no matter what happened, she would see this through.

Two more weeks!

So depressing.

98

Midnite

Dear Universe,

My eye continues plague me. Every four hours without fail the Allen and my April would catch me, hold me, and torture me with the dreaded eye drops. I know I was not cooperating. I always gave my most ferocious growl while trying to bite the Allen as hard as I could. I didn't want to but he left me no choice.

My April proved to be really sneaky. She would sneak around coming up behind me putting the terrible drops in my damaged eye. If only I could make them stop.

Anubis would talk to me about the biting. He felt I was being a brat, while not appreciating what they were doing for me.

Pawprints To The Universe

I could hear that Eros upstairs who assaulted me. The April said she was keeping us separate for now.

For now?

Eros should be thrown out of here for the violence upon me. I was suffering because of him….. and no I was not a bad boy here. The stupid cat had teased me into barking so loud at him. I am the victim here! I am the one injured and I am the one with this huge collar who can't scratch his itchy eye. The feline fur ball was the bad one. How about for now I won't beat him up like he did me?

Okay. I know, I know.

There are no victims. That sounds stupid to me. All I did was tell Eros off. He responded by ripping my eye out. Where's the justice here?

Ok.

Ok.

Ok.

I will try to be forgiving. I will not be a brat, but right now if I saw Eros I would have a hard time forgiving.

Yes. Yes.

I know that's how it works. The April says that in a few days we were going back to the doctor. The collar was beyond miserable. My April held my water bowl close so I could drink. She scooped my food on her fingers so I could just lick it off.

If it had not been for my April I would have starved to death. It was easier now that we had a routine, but I still kept bumping into things.

I pray every night dear Universe that I can take this stupid thing off. My April feels bad I can tell, but she keeps mumbling about tough love.

Apparently I could mess up the surgery if I touch it. That was so hard because it itched like crazy. Yes. I know that's a good thing, but it's so annoying.

Pawprints To The Universe

Every night my April would sleep on the couch so we could be together….. just the two of us.

I would sleep next to her, trying to be comfortable in the collar. It was a while after the eye drop torture that I felt it get a little looser. If I stretched my paw I could slip my claw into the small space.

I know dear Universe that I shouldn't do it. I knew I could get in trouble. However it felt so good to rub my claw across my cheek It felt like it had been 100 years that the collar had been on me.

Patiently I kept wiggling until the ties started to untangle. Once I started I couldn't stop. I knew I should, but it felt so good to finally touch the itch.

"GUINNESS! Nooooo!"

Oh! No!

My April had awakened Boy was she ever mad! She grabbed me holding my front paws away from my face. She yelled for the Allen who came running. Oh boy. Was I ever in trouble.

"Guinness! Honey! You can't take the collar off! How did you get your paw in there? Oh my god! Whatever you do, do <u>NOT</u> touch your eye!"

She held me down, which was so unnecessary. I was only going to scratch it a little bit. The Allen sat down next to us whispering in my ear to be a good puppy!

I <u>am</u> a good puppy! It's been pure torture to keep this on! Certainly I could take it off now.

My paw was stuck. The collar began to twist practically choking me to death. I couldn't help but go into bite mode. The Allen was trying to get my paw out. My April was crying, worried that I would mess my eye up. I had teeth and I knew how to use them. The Allen had his secret weapon called cooking mitts. He put them on as I tried to bite his intruding fingers off. This was torture! Why were they both being so mean to me? I'm an injured puppy! Dear Universe. Save me!

For a midnite debacle this was a big one. My leg felt like it was going to break. The collar was tight.

I was going to choke! I gave the oven mitt my best chomp. While I held on hoping to hurt him to make him stop, my leg came loose from the collar. All three of us collapsed on the couch. My April quickly tightened the neck and I was a prisoner yet again.

Would this torture never end!

By this time I was very sleepy. I just wanted to nestle into my April's arms. For a brief moment I thought all would be well. The then the Allen says...

"Oh no! It's been four hours. We have to do the eye drops!"

Both he and my April sighed deeply.

"I'll go get the drops", said my April.

"I'll be here with our resident velociraptor", replied Allen.

These two were relentless. Couldn't they cut me a break this time?

My April returned while the Allen gripped me tightly. I could fight it of course, but I was so tired. My teeth gripped his hands as tightly as I could muster. The drops burned into my eye, making me so uncomfortable. I just gave up. Tough love? Yeah. Tough love. My April held me close. The Allen left the room, which meant I had four more hours until they tortured me again.

Would this never end?

99

Starting To Feel Better

Dear Universe,

Six weeks is a very long time for a puppy to endure tough love. Every day my eye is starting to feel better. I could feel the sting of the drops less and less.

My April was always wondering if I could still see out of my eye. At first I wasn't sure because of the pain. Now I could see just fine. If I could get this stupid collar off all would be well. When will we go back to the doctor? I didn't know. It was actually kind of cool to eat off my April's fingers. Somehow it tasted better that way. She also seemed to know when I was thirsty. The water bowl was lifted up to my snout. All I had to do was lap it up. So at least I was not going to die of hunger or thirst.

Why does my eye take so long to heal dear Universe? Shouldn't it just happen real fast? I have tried to be patient but tough love is almost impossible to get through. There's got to be a better way.

I know.

I know.

I should be grateful I did not lose my eye. That little cat did a lot of damage to me. Isn't he going to get his? Will he?

Wait a second.

Why do I have to forgive him? He deliberately scratched my eye?

Okay.

Okay.

No I don't get it.

Okay. Yes I did yell at him. No I didn't scare him!

Oh.

I did?

Oh.

But he's not hurt! I am!

Okay.

I have to find forgiveness in my heart. I have to be a big puppy and let it go.

Gosh. That's going to be so hard dear Universe. My April says she is going to keep us separate so it never happens again. Isn't that enough?

No?

Geez…..

100

Collar Off!

Dear Universe,

Today is a glorious day! This morning I found ut
we were going to see the doctor. Hopefully this
means I can get this collar off. I haven't been able to
do much since the incident. I really need to stretch
my legs!

We left early to get to Pasadena. I sat up in the
front seat next to my April. My view was obstructed
again because of the stupid collar. Gosh. I could
hardly wait to get there.

When we walked in there were a lot of dogs
there. One in particular was a male Pug whose name
was Lars. Both of his eyes were cloudy. He sat with
his nose in the air. I asked him what he was sniffing.
He turned to look at me and I realized he could not
see me. So cloudy his eyes were.

"I am sniffing so I can see what's here in my head. Our sniffers are more powerful than our eyes. Mine are pretty shot now, so I use my sniffer. You should be thankful you can still see my friend", said Lars.

I told him of being attacked by Eros the cat. My hatred for him made Lars shake his head.

"My friend, you have to forgive him. Otherwise your energy will continue to suffer."

Now I thought about this dear Universe. How does forgiveness fix everything? Especially when I was the one so damaged. Is it really necessary?

I see.

Ok.

So I told Lars it was a good idea. Just then a girl came into the room and called my name. I was up and running before my April could even stand up! She laughed at my excitement. I think she was excited too. It had been a long haul but we were finally at the finish line.

We sat in the examining room with me in my April's lap. I felt safe there. I anticipated a meltdown if I had to keep wearing the collar. I think my April knew that too.

I could feel her fingers scratching my back. It did relax me a little. The door knob turned and there she was. The doctor.

"Well Mr. Guinness. Let's get a look at that eye!"

She shined a light at me. It made me blink a lot. It worried me that she would find a reason for me to keep the collar on.

"Well Guinness, it's all looking good! See what tough love can do?"

With that she undid the collar.

Oh my God!

What a relief!

I could lick my April's face again!

Yay!

My April carried me to the car in celebration. I sat on her lap nestled in her energy. I'm glad this tough love thing is over. It's not something that's easy. I am going to consider forgiveness. Because I know you want me to dear Universe.

The hum of the car motor felt so good. I am a lucky puppy.

101

Intruder Alert

Dear Universe,

I have been in charge here for quite a few years now. My confidence returned with great force a while back. I have a lot of responsibility taking care of my April. She and I are soul mates on a lot of levels. I know that there can be many good matches you taught me that. However I never met anyone who even came close. I am thankful that she rescued me for I fear I would have allowed myself to die. It would have been an escape from a sad life with no love. The Maha brought my April and I together, or was it you dear Universe?

The big dogs have all gone home to you having had wonderful lives after they were rescued. I am the only puppy left which suites me just fine. Having to be in charge of all the kittens is a big job but I am up for it.

Every night I snuggle deep into the soft blankets remembering when I was cold and wet. If only I could have shared this with Blade. He's with you now so take good care of him. I think he would be proud of what I have accomplished since I've been here. Being in charge makes me feel good. I want it all forever ever ever!

Luckily I have never run into Eros the wicked cat again. My April keeps us separate for our own good she says. The other cats stay clear especially when it's time for me to discipline the group. So basically I am the only puppy. The only critter of value since I am the only puppy.

One morning my April got up early leaving without me. I went by the Allen to sit with him so he wouldn't be lonely. Maybe if he got hungry he might make steak, so it was necessary to stay close. Just in case I could talk him into giving me some.

It was really weird that the Allen could not feel my thoughts as I stared at him. Was he ignoring me? OR maybe he just didn't have any steak. Steak should be kept in the cold box all the time.

So with great disappointment I fell back asleep watching TV (the talking box). I tried to keep one eye open but the blankets were too soft.

I heard the phone ring and the Allen answered. The conversation went like this.

"Hey Babe….. oh….. oh no….. are you sure?.... Ok….. Just bring her here. I'll make sure Guinness is secure….."

Secure??!! What the heck does that mean? I glared at him as he got up off the couch.

"G!"

"Come in G!"

"Let's go in the office."

"Come on boy…"

Why do I have to go to the office? My April wasn't there so why go?

Pawprints To The Universe

He stood in the doorway all impatient.

What was going on?

I didn't authorize anyone to put me in the office. Well I just was not going to do it. I am a smart puppy. No one fools me. So we stood facing each other. The Allen trying to talk me into something I did not want to do. I started to bark a lot trying to let him know I was NOT going in there. This was all too suspicious. The Allen left the room. A few seconds later he returned with my most favorite thing..... a Greenie..... boy he sure doesn't play fair!

Oh Ok! The office it is! Fork over my Greenie first.

There.

Thank you.

Ok now maybe I will go into the office. Just remember I know when something is up. Something is definitely going in.

As the door shut I sat down to enjoy my Greenie. I could hear commotion but at the moment my treat was the most important.

I heard the door open and close. My April must have returned. Why wasn't she outraged at my containment?

I gave a few question barks but no response. There was a lot of commotion. What were they doing? Maybe they didn't hear me. I tried jumping at the door while giving my best bark. One that indicated I wasn't happy.

Nothing.

With agitation I picked up my Greenie while guarding the door. I thought the treat would make me feel better but it didn't.

The I hear it!

I couldn't believe my ears?

Oh no!

I must get out of this room. Oh dear Universe, I heard a small weak bark. A bark!!

An intruder??!!

I must escape! We are being invaded. The Allen and my April might be in grave danger.

Grrrr.

Suddenly the door opened. There was my April! Whew! She was ok. What's going on?

She sat in one of the chairs.

"I have something to tell you Guinness", she said.

My heart started beating real fast. What was she going to tell me?

Bad news!

"I have brought home a scared puppy that's going to be your new sister."

Sister?

Oh, no.

"Now you be nice G. She's had a rough time. She is scared and hungry. I'm counting on you to welcome her here. She needs our help."

Oh dear Universe! How can I deal with this? I liked being the only puppy. We don't need any more puppies. I am your only puppy!

There she was being held by the Allen.

TRAITOR!

Boy was I mad! I could smell her scent. It was true. She was really scared. I was worried it was all a scam. Sometimes critters will lie to get food or shelter. I know it happens. I have been there.

Yeah yeah! I know.

I should be sharing my good fortune, but I am her one and only. I don't want to share.

Pawprints To The Universe

Just then I saw her lick the Allen's face. What a suck up!

I searched her eyes, trying to find a good reason to hate her. Just showing up was enough reason.

I barked so much my April hugged me tightly. She told me the same thing you did.

Be nice to her. She's had a rough time. Her human died. She needs a new home. Blah Blah Blah! We don't need any new puppies here!

102

Little Bit

Dear Universe,

Good grief! What a drama queen this Little Bit is. She's playing all the right cards. Acting all innocent and afraid. My April is buying this stuff!

What am I going to do?

Last night my April spent the night on the couch with me. The little intruder was sequestered in a small fenced area very close to the couch. I made sure I slept right above my April's head, on part of the pillow.

Jeez!

My April whispered in my ear on how I was the love of her life. No one would ever be above me. Well, of course. Afterall, I am Guinness. Okay, the intruder can stay. First time she gives me any trouble….. out she goes.

Ok dear Universe, I know that's not very nice, but my April is my April. That needs to be understood. The little intruder. I could see she was working her way towards the couch every day. Couldn't they see that?

Oh good grief! There she goes again, doing a little whimper. Next comes the little tap dance followed by the cutesy little bark.

So manipulative!

So crafty!

Can't anyone see this but me?

Ok dear Universe, I'll stop. I don't see why I have to share my good fortune. There's a whole bunch, I know. I also know a crafty intruder when I see one.

Ok.

It finally happened. I have come nose to nose with her. My April picked her up and brought her over to me.

You both need to become friends", she said. "You have a lot more in common than you think you do."

Oh boy. My April is falling for her lies. I tried to tell her but she said we needed to help her. So grow up and be a big brother. Ok?

"I'll make nice if you will", whispered Little Bit.

She must have missed my eye rolling, which thankfully I was still able to do after my brutal attack by Eros. She threw herself on the floor showing me her belly. Wow. The ultimate surrender. She then spoke that she agreed I was the boss. I was number one. With that she remained on her back looking up at me with those goofy eyes.

My April, of course, was impressed with Bit's submission. She was maybe right about this working out. Maybe I can turn the intruder into a staunch supporter. Maybe I will be nice.

103

My Pillow

Dear Universe,

Okay, being nice only works for a little while. I know you told me in my gratefulness I should share the opportunity with others. This is really hard though. I was here first. It's a real fact that I am number one. If the little intruder wants to stay she needs to support me in all things.

It first became obvious that Little Bit/Intruder was lying through her little snout. My April finally took down the fenced containment area. She was invited to come sleep in the couch with us. Naturally I expected to have my spot on the pillow. I was detained because I was getting a drink. When I returned the intruder was already there, sleeping in my spot on the pillow.

Outrageous!

I started yelling at her to get out of my spot! Can you believe she did not open her eyes. She was pretending to sleep so she would not have to move.

NOT OKAY!

The barking got really loud as my April came back into the room. "Guinness, Guinness, Guinness! You are not being nice", she exclaimed.

Couldn't she see that I was upset? This little intruder stole my spot right after I told her what the rules were.

Yeah dear Universe, I know I should share….. but share my April!?? I don't think so! I am not being unreasonable am I? Let the intruder get her own soul mate!

Ok, if you think I'm being a brat you have a right to your opinion. Just trying to protect my turf.

What? You want me to apologize!

No way!

Why do I have to say I'm sorry? I didn't do anything! She should be the one to apologize!

Not me!

My April sat between us trying to cool down the situation. She said again how much Little Bit had suffered.

"How would you feel if I passed away?" she said.

Yeah. I'd be pretty unhappy, but I would not try to steal someone else's love!

During our conversation Little Bit woke up. There was no snotty remarks made and for a second I thought maybe I should let her sleep on the pillow. On second thought, I realize that she could wreck my pillow. Maybe she could sleep by the foot while I got the pillow.

My April calmed us both down. Little Bit did not get snarky. I did, but was quickly silenced. I got my spot on the pillow. Little Bit got a blanket wrapped around her at the other end.

Pawprints To The Universe

My April said she needed to feel safe. She was not here to take my place. A safe place for her was what was happening here.

Yes dear Universe, I know I am not the only puppy on the planet. What do you want from me? I am trying to have more of a heart. Just realize that until I got to Maha and April I lost my heart along the way. Guess it just comes from great loss, but I do want to be a good puppy.

So….. OK….. she can sleep with us!

There.

Happy now?

Just know that if she gets possessive I will bite her in the butt! Okay. Sorry. I will just yell at her. Getting situated on the couch took a little time and adjustment. In the end, Bit slept by my April's feet and I got my pillow.

Certainly I got some growth credit for this. What do you think dear Universe?

Pawprints To The Universe

As much as I don't want to admit it, Little Bit is kind of cute. I plan now to train her to be my slave or something. I'm certainly not going to share my food with her. She will just have to adjust to my reality.

I curled up next to my April. If I reached my paw out I could touch her cheek. So cool.

104

VERONICA

Dear Universe,

Boy am I confused?

I spend every day now at the feet of my April. My supervision of her day is my first priority. I'm lucky that she doesn't leave the house to go to work. Not sure what she does, but I am confused.

I know her scent, that never changes. However sometimes it's like she is someone else. Her energy shifted as well. I asked her one day what was going on? I growled at this other energy then felt bad cuz I could clearly see it looked like my April.

She said there is a spirt named Veronica that she lets speak through her.

What?

That explains it. It made me think a lot. She said that this Veronica helped people.

Okay.

Once this Veronica even talked to me. So weird because it looked like my April. Smelled like my April, and the hands that scratched my ears were hers too. The energy felt so different that it confused me a little.

So dear Universe you did not tell me about this new development. My April lets spirit speak through her. Hopefully she will always come back. It's not that I do not like this spirit, it's just that I love love love my April. It's just one more thing I will have to manage.

I was invited to blend and experience for myself. At first I was shy. It felt weird but I felt that this other being was cool and that she liked me. It's different to sit on her lap but I can feel the difference.

So not really scary at all. It's part of my job now to sit with my April as she does this.

What is it called?

Oh yeah! Channeling.

Hey dear Universe, are you involved with this? I think you must be as this energy is warm and fuzzy like you.

In all the years since I've been here I've never missed a session. The times I cannot go always makes me sad. I just want to be with my April as much as possible.

I sit at her feet all the time. This energy is called VERONICA. She's always nice to me. I love her a lot but of course every one and every thing are not as good as my April.

Sometimes I lift up out of body to go with her traveling. The first time I was a little scared but now I look forward to being with her in that way.

So cool.

Pawprints To The Universe

You know dear Universe, I never would have thought that when I was under that old porch, that someday I would be flying around in other places. I think the word is dimensions.

So cool.

I guess life can take you to places you never imagined. I remember wanting to find someone. Wasn't sure why I was on this planet. At the time, nothing was going well. I do remember seeing my April's face when I was sleeping. In those dreams we would be together laughing. We are often in different places, but always together.

At the time I was too young to figure it out. All I needed was to survive. Food, shelter, and love were missing, so I had to go find it. Now that I'm more grown up and not worried about survival, I understand these things better.

Never did I ever think I would find the woman with the golden hair. Never did I think I would have enough food or experience a soft touch.

Never.

So to actually find her. To be transported to a new world and life had to be from you dear Universe.

My purpose now is to live and breathe my new life.

So cool.

105

Pigs from Guinea

Dear Universe,

One of the many new experiences of living in this place called California was the introduction to other life forms. The house that my April lives in has a multitude of animals, some I never knew existed.

This brings me to the little critters in the plastic pool. There were only a few when I got here, but they seemed to have multiplied a lot since then.

They are kept in a small room that is called the porch. At first I thought they were mice but they did not have tails. I came to find out that they were pigs from Guinea. Not sure where Guinea is, but wherever they come from they are so annoying. It appears they have no order in their lives. I have to bark my head off to get them to listen to me. If they do it's because they are hiding in one of their huts. They should know better than to ignore me.

Most of the time they are kept by themselves on the porch. At first there were only about 5 of them. Recently there seems to be a lot more of them. I asked my April what was going on. She said that some of them were lying about being boys. How could that be? It all sounded really shady.

I guess it's all about the birds and the bees stuff I've heard about. It just seems that every time I turn around they are 10 more. Pretty soon they will over populate this house. They simply do not listen. What can a puppy do dear Universe?

What?

What do you mean? Are you saying that I don't listen either? Of course I do!

I always listen! It's these ornery pigs who do not! It drives me crazy into a vicious circle of misbehavior because I have to keep repeating myself until I am screaming. If I scream then my April tells me I have to calm down!

Yes I know this is a much bigger problem than just me. These pigs simply refuse to cooperate. Drives me crazy.

Oh, okay. I drive you crazy? I always listen to you! Don't I?

Oh ok! So I don't listen very well either. Are you saying that if I start listening better the pigs will start to listen better?

Ok.

I will try.

In the meantime, I have to yell at them. Last week I stuck my head in their hut. Told them all off pretty well. They are cute and will squeal back at me if I push to hard.

I wonder why my April has such little creatures in her possession. There are so many. I make an effort every day to listen. I really do, but I guess I need to try harder.

It's difficult to listen when you have so much to say. The pigs most likely will never listen to anyone. So I think your advice will not work in this situation.

In the meantime, I get a kick out of yelling at the pigs. My April tells me that I am scaring them. They don't look scared to me. However I do stop when she tells me to, but I try to get as much discipline in as possible every day.

My April says there are so many because the boys pretended to be girls when she first got them. So dear Universe, how does a boy masquerade as a girl? This place is so confusing. Boys should be boys. Girls should be girls. How you can pretend is more than I can get as a puppy.

106

Tutu

Dear Universe,

Sometimes I know I get a little out of control. Often the cats try to annoy me on purpose. The big bird in the cage can talk like a human. How does he do it? His name is Tutu. He sits in the room where the box of humans is. Every day he watches a program where an announcer screams "come on down". There's lots of chaos and commotion. Tutu literally rocks out during the music, then also screams "come on down". It's really annoying when one is trying to nap.

In an effort to make him be quiet I joined in with a lot of barking. It didn't work.

All it got me was my April shushing me instead of the bird! So not fair!

I know I should be nicer but Tutu is really smart. Almost as smart as me! I guess I have to be more quiet cuz all the noise troubles my April. So okay. I will try to be nicer but someone needs to talk to this cockatoo.

I am finding that being in charge is hard. All the cats ignore my commands, often jumping ono my back to shut me up. If I bark my April tells me to be nice.

So frustrating!

I know dear Universe that I am one lucky puppy. All of my dreams have come true. Now it's my job to help out around here. If left to their own devices the cats would wreak havoc on this household. It's exhausting to keep them all disciplined and under control. I think they laugh at me behind my back. They steal my food! I get hysterical when they won't listen. My April will come to pick me up before I have a meltdown. It was a great excuse to sit on her lap to be comforted. I readily admit that sometimes I get upset on purpose because of all the attention I get.

107

Skunk, Aliens, and Death Rays

Dear Universe,

Now that I have been here a while I am starting to realize how messed up this world is. I see the humans being mean to each other, failing to love as they should.

Here in my home I feel the need to protect everyone (including the pigs) safe. It feels like there are evil forces afoot. As long as I am in charge here I will do my best to keep everyone safe.

It's important for a puppy to have a purpose. Since I have settled in I am becoming more and more courageous.

It was a Saturday morning that my bravery came into question. An incident happened where I had to show everyone what I was made of.

Every Saturday morning my April would go to teach dance to little humans. I know because she had taken me to class a few times. I got antsy trying to be quiet so I decided that it would be better if I stayed home.

So before my April would leave she would take me out for my morning pee. The door opened and I ran out. At first I did not see it. While I was doing a thorough sniff, there it was.

Was it a cat?

No!

Was it a dog?

No!

Well what was this creature? Of course it was necessary to investigate. Maybe it was an alien or something. It was black with a white stripe running down its back. Maybe it was friendly. Maybe I should try to communicate with it. I slowly moved forward looking for signs of recognition.

Closer.

Closer.

Closer

Aarrgh!

Oh my God!

It's spraying me with a mist! What is this?

It's burning my eyes! I think I just swallowed some of it.

Aarrgh!!

I started running in circles. The death ray was circling around me. It smelled bad! The more I ran the more it hurt my eyes. I started to bark hysterically. Coming all this way to find my true love only to be destroyed by a death ray from an alien was not okay.

My April came running out into the small courtyard. I was relieved to see her. Maybe she could save me! Maybe she would send this creature back to whatever planet in came from.

"Oh my God Guinness! Get away from the skunk! Guinness! Get away from the skunk!"

Oh! So that is what this creature is. It's death ray was completely over powering. I might choke and die leaving my April all alone and vulnerable to this alien monster!

"Guinness! You stink little boy! The skunk just sprayed you to protect itself. It even squirted me!"

My April was upset! This was not okay. I wanted to fix it, but was fearful of this death ray!

"Guinness get in the house! Stop trying to protect me! I have to go to work. I have to change clothes! You need to cooperate my friend. In the house..... NOW!"

Pawprints To The Universe

When my April was like this I learned not to argue. I smelled bad? If it's just a stink I can handle it.

"No Guinness!   <u>Do NOT</u> get on the couch. Please come here. We need to give you a bath!"

A bath? I don't think so. It doesn't smell that bad. Does it?   Dear Universe, how does this happen!? I really don't like baths. Why do these skunks exist? Are they really from another planet? I think they are. Now they are trying to abduct me, I am sure of it.

My April soaped me up and squirted water right in my face. This is not acceptable. These aliens are crafty, even if they are called skunks.

The warm water on my back did feel good. If I wasn't so upset the massage would feel great. I am so unhappy right now.   Should be thankful I survived the attack I guess! We need to rid the world of these barbarians. Adding "saving the world" to my list of important things to do?

Pawprints To The Universe

What do you mean dear Universe? You say I am blowing it all out of proportion. How is that so?

This alien skunk came into my yard and attacked me! NO! It wasn't scared! It had an agenda of destruction. My April said the stink would probably stay with me for a while. For a while? Good grief, totally ruined my life! How is this fair?

My April took a bottle of red juice and poured it all over me. Wasn't getting a bath in the kitchen sink with all the stupid cats in the audience enough?

I have to ask dear Universe..... why is this happening?

108

The Aliens Exit

Dear Universe,

I have survived the alien attack! The red liquid my April poured on me smells terrible. It's also sticky. Oily fur looks all gooey. The cats are rolling on the floor with laughter. So embarrassing!

As soon as I finished my bath I ran over to the window to see if the aliens were still there.

Nope!

Nowhere in sight?

Well I must have scared them off. Now I had to maintain their exit, keeping them away from my new home. No stupid skunk was going to mess with an attack dog like me…..

Pawprints To The Universe

Hey!

Dear Universe stop laughing. I can be vicious and fearless when faced with alien death rays. My April just thinks they are skunks. What if they are really from another planet? What if they are here to spray all of us with their death rays?

I rolled around on the floor rug trying to dry off. I really hate baths but I just had to suck it up and do it. My April left to go teach her classes, leaving me to monitor the aliens. I planted myself right in the window. It is really important I stay in view of them should they decide to return.

109

Multiplication

Dear Universe,

So as I said, I am disciplining the pigs. My April watches me closely so I must be gentle. Today was confusing because I could have sworn there were about 20 of them. Now there is at least 30? What is going on here?

I tried to alert my April but she couldn't understand me because I was barking too fast! There is growing suspicion that they are going to take over the world. At least that is what they said!

My April sat with me while I tried to explain this problem. Lucky for me she was patient. It took me a few minutes but I finally convince her to come take a look!

"OH my god G! Someone had a few babies…..
AGAIN!"

I knew they couldn't be trusted. Somehow they
managed to create more of them. Now my April
says there are 30 of them!

30!!?

Are they using magic or something? I asked why
they did that. My April said it had something to do
with the birds and the bees?! I don't see any birds
and the bees are outside! They are not in the house.
Why is everybody putting the blame on them? It's
obviously a huge pig thing. Sometimes I think my
April doesn't know why things are the way they are.
I get that! BUT!! This looks like a takeover plot of
some kind. I remember when Blade and I were
under the porch, there were mice who did the same
thing. They would try to steal what little food we
had. I spent many a night scaring them off of our
stolen food. No fair that they were stealing it from
us!

Any ways.

Pigs appear to be as crafty as mice. A little cuter because they have fluffy fur. Their intent so obvious. Steal the puppy food. I have to talk my April into getting rid of them. Or if she doesn't want to do that, then she should let me train them. It would be a pleasure to force them to behave. Alas she said no!

Why?

She said that it wasn't the new baby pigs' fault. It was hers. So if I wanted to yell at someone I should yell at her.

Really?

My April. How could I ever yell at her? Well maybe if she tries to give me a bath..... then maybe. Otherwise it would be a big fat no!

I wondered how she was going to handle these new piggies. I thought they should know I am in charge as soon as possible. That way I could train them not to multiply themselves. I could let them know they need to look to me as their leader. Maybe they should also listen to me when I bark! At the

Pawprints To The Universe

very least! I'm still trying to figure out how they did it. There are 6 new ones. They are teeny tiny, but I'm sure they will grow up to be a problem. So it's really important to train them now!

110

Boys and Girls

Dear Universe,

Well my April and the Diane took each pig today through an exam. She said they needed to figure out who were boys and who were girls.

Ok.

How does one do that?

I watched them both as they put girls in one area and boy in the other.

Is this really a good idea?

I'm still trying to figure out what the birds and bees have to do with it. I guess at some point it will reveal itself. Right now it's a big mystery. I was just glad they let me stay in the room while they did it.

Why are their guinea pigs dear Universe? They don't listen. They make silly noises and just run around their habitat. Eat and poop mostly. Do they have a real purpose for being here? Or are they just having fun? I know if they listened to me I could teach them how to do things for me.

I have all these plans for the pigs but my favorite part is chasing them around. I know it's kind of mean but it's just so much fun to see them run away. One of them even yells back at me! My April says if I want to yell it's better than touching.

No touching.

I get it.

It's hard to be a good boy all the time!

My April says that there should not be anymore babies. She and Diane have verified who is who and what is what. So they say. As for me I will continue to discipline whenever I get the chance.

I know. I know.

Being in charge does not permit me to be abusive. Although it's hard not to bark right in their stupid faces.

What?

I can't call them stupid?

Why not?

Oh. Okay. Just because someone is having a different experience than you it's ot okay to judge them. But But But!

What if they are acting stupid?

What then?

Oh.

I see.

Dear Universe I am trying to be good. I know that I can be snarky. I also know how lucky I am to have found my place in this world. It's all turned out way better than what it was under that porch.

I won't call them names but if they are being stupid then I should be able to express myself.

What?

Okay,, I will make every effort to be nice..... even if they are stupid.

111

Bees

Dear Universe,

Okay today I have one big question. Well maybe 2 questions. Why oh why did you create bees? And what do bees have to do with guinea pigs? They are vile creatures that lay in wait to sting poor unsuspecting puppies. The first time I ran into one it looked like it was in trouble. On the floor buzzing in circles. I decided to investigate. My snout sniffed gently trying to determine what the problem was. Just as I got close the mean creature stuck his stinger right on my mouth.

OUCH!

Oh my god! For something so little it sure has a big stinger. It hurt sooooo bad! Running around the room hoping it would stop, I found that my snout was getting bigger.

My April responded to my cries immediately. It was hard for me to bark or anything.

"Your mouth is swollen G! Did you get stung by a bee?!" she exclaimed.

Yes! I was viciously attacked when I tried to see if it was okay! All I got for my efforts was a big stinger in my snout. It really hurts a lot. What an ungrateful creature!

I could feel weird stuff happening in my mouth. It felt like I had a mouthful of yucky food. In a panic I jumped into my April's arms. She cradled me in her arms while I howled in pain. Would it ever stop!

Oh no!

I can hardly open my mouth. Surly I will die.

What if my mouth swells shut?

What if my snout falls off?

Pawprints To The Universe

What if I am transformed into a bee myself? I heard that if a vampire bites you there is a possibility that I would turn into a vampire.

What if that happens to me? The next thing I knew my April was trying to put a pill down my throat.

Oh no!

I am not swallowing it!

Oh my dear Universe, I may be coming to you very soon. If my snout doesn't stop getting bigger I may die! Just when I get everything I ever wanted I will die tragically by a bee bite! It's so unfair!

While I was crying my April brought some liquid in a dropper towards me. What? No thank you! It's yucky!

Please don't make it go in my mouth!

My April was persistent. She managed to get the liquid in my mouth. It tastes terrible. My tongue feels numb! My snout smells funny cuz a few drops landed in my fur! I may die this day!

Okay dear Universe! Maybe I am being too dramatic <u>but</u> it hurts so bad. I can't even drink water because my tongue forgot how to. I ate some kibble but it tasted like the medicine too. I drooled all over the place. Am I gonna die?

"No! You are not", said my April. "It's medicine and it will make the swelling go down. You should be okay in a little bit".

A little bit?

You know dear Universe, why do things take so long? Why can't everything happen just like that?

Why?

My snout did begin to feel better. My April held me the whole time, which felt wonderful. I am really mad at that stupid bee. He should have listened to me instead of trying to kill me!

Pawprints To The Universe

Getting my ears scratched helped pass the time until the swelling in my snout went down. Finally my tongue felt normal again. Maybe it would be possible to get a little food in my tummy. Maybe. The other animals in the house thought I was being a big baby. Even Anubis told me I was.

Geesh!

None of them got stung! How is it that they know everything? I was attacked! Can't anyone see that?

What?

What dear Universe?

Heal yourself and carry on?

Carry on?

I am not playing victim!

I am a victim! I was attacked!

I know that I am strong now.

I know that I am in charge of how my life goes.

BUT!

How does one not be a victim when you *are* a victim?

Oh.

Oh I see.

I guess I was looking for revenge. The bee hurt me though. His stinger really hurt. So what am I supposed to do with that?

What?

Are you kidding?

Forgive the bee?

It was just trying to protect itself?

Wait a second! I did not sting the bee….. it stung me!

Oh.

Oh I see.

It thought I was attacking him?

I was just sniffing to see what he was up to and then…..

BAM!

He stung me.

So you're saying that this is a misunderstanding?

Oh no.

He deliberately stung me.

Stupid bee.

Oh ok.

I will stop talking like that.   Still do not understand this whole victim thing.

As I snuggled with my April my heart calmed down a lot. Yes I know I am a lucky puppy. By sniffing too close I upset the bee, but he didn't have to sting me. I guess that's the way of misunderstanding. So reacting with more barking and yelling I will try to make peace with the bee by trying to understand how he views the world.

Ok.

That makes more sense. A lot of arguing and hurt can be stopped by walking in the paw prints of others. Even if it's just for a moment.

Ok I get it.

So dear Universe, my question now is….. why don't humans do that? Most of what I have seen does not look very good.

The mother always told me to be careful of humans. If you're lucky enough to find find a good one it's a good idea to hold on to him/her. Not everyone is so lucky.

I look up at my April with peace. Forgiveness is a good thing. So ok. I forgive the bee cause it was just scared. I get that. Maybe the rest of the humans should think about that.

I know most would say I am just a dog. A silly dog that does not know as much as a human. That's not true. I am finding I know now that I am just using this form. I am a piece of you dear Universe.

That's kind of cool!

Now where's that treat you were talking about? A greenie would be good. Out of all the treats, that one is my favorite.

112

Greenies

Dear Universe,

Well I have been here with my April for quite sometime. It's been better than I could have imagined! She feeds me, loves me, and watches out for me. A true blue loving relationship. No worries anymore for a puppy like me. So it worried me a little when big globs of my hair started falling out.

FLEAS!!

Oh no. I had fleas once before at the shelter Blade and I were in. They put this horrible smelly stuff on me that almost made me choke. My eyes watered for days afterward. Please my dear April, don't put that stuff on me. Please don't. Of course she considered putting flea poison on me!

Pawprints To The Universe

Fortunately she decided to just give me a bath in the kitchen sink. The water was warm and she massaged the flea shampoo into my body. It actually felt good!

While she was drying me off with a towel she remarked that some of my fur was falling off. She did not like that!

Neither did I.

I hoped that the bath would be the end of it. Should have known that a trip to the vet would be the next thing she would arrange.

So the next morning we got in the car for my appointment. The vet was a nice guy. He always treated me nicely. He took a good look at my fairly hairless body and said he thought it was allergies of some kind. He said there were a lot of tests that he could do to find out what I was allergic to. It did not sound like a lot of fun.

My April told him that she did not want to put me through all that. Was there any other way?

The vet said she would have to monitor my food intake everyday while eliminating different foods. That sounds like a plan!

So when we went home "the diet" began. First thing was taking me off grains.

Grains!

I'm eating grains! As far as I know I eat all meaty stuff out of those cans. My April promised to run the little food tests so I would not even know I was being tested. That was pretty cool.

My hair loss continued as we experimented. Finally we had eliminated just about everything. The only things left were my treats. It made me nervous to think that one of them may have been the culprit.

Oh dear Universe, did I every tell you about the Greenies? They are the best treats I ever ever had. They were of course green in color and ever so tasty. It was one of the first new things in my new life. They became an obsession for me. There was never a time when I did not want one. So when my April announced that we would not have any Greenies for one month I was sad.

My fur was a disaster. I only had hair on my head and tail. Very little anywhere else. The cats were always teasing me about how stupid they thought I looked. It wasn't my fault! It just fell out! My April said I was still a handsome guy. So having hair really did not matter to me.

The first day of no Greenies was pure torture. I don't know how many times I begged her for one. She, of course, was very strict. What would it matter if I had just a teeny weeny piece!?

It was a long month. By the end of it some of my hair had started to grow back. On no! Does this mean that I'm allergic to Greenies! It must be some sort of mistake! Greenies are my most favorite food ever! What will happen if all my hair comes back? Does that mean I don't get any Greenies anymore?

The month flew by and my hair did start to grow back. Darn! Just when I found the perfect treat!

Pawprints To The Universe

To this day I still miss them. Maybe I could have just agreed to be hairless. A world with no Greenies is not bright. My April said no more greenies! Darn! Why is life so unfair dear Universe?

113

Conclusions

Dear Universe,

I sat next to my April today thinking about my life now. I know that some humans are bad. I used to think they all were. Somehow I managed to find a few good ones.

It began with the mean one adopting me so long ago. Now she was an example of a bad, however she led me to Maha who tried to rescue me from her clutches. It was the first time I was treated with love by a human. She even remembered to feed me and let me outside to pee. It was confusing at first but I soon realized that love felt way better than hate. I guess dear Universe it was my first big lesson.

"Always pick love".

I get that now. The mean one no longer lives on this planet, so I hear. That means she must be with you. For all the mean things she did to me I hope she knows better now. At the time I was really mad at her..... and hurt that she did not appear to love me. I didn't know at the time why she was so mean. I thought I had done something wrong. No, that wasn't the case. Now the truth of her own despair is available I can feel sadness for her that she felt the need to react to my love with all the negativity she could muster.

Take care of her dear Universe. Teach her what love is. Maybe if I ever see her again she will be nicer.

I used to think I was an unlucky puppy while living under the porch with my brother Blade. Now I know that I am actually a very lucky puppy. It took a while but I found my human. My April. Without Maha that would not have happened. I send puppy kisses everyday to her. I hope she feels them.

All of the other dogs I have met along the way have also taught me a lot. First there was Shannon and Tory. I think Tory is the one who influenced me the most. He was never shy about pointing out my somewhat stupid decisions. Without him I may have turned into a bitter puppy. He shared his human with me so that I could escape the mean one. All in all, pretty cool.

There was when I arrived in California the chows who were the puppies of my April before I got there. They also taught me a lot. Their names were Tata and Anubis. Both of them had homelessness issues until my April rescued them. So they both understood my plight.

There was also a chow named RA. He was a magical puyppy so said Tata and Anubis. Apparently he knew you pretty well dear Universe. I never got the chance to meet him but the stories shared by the others tell me he and I would have been friends as well. He came to you before I ever got here. His presence influenced all of us. When I come to see you dear Universe I hope I can meet him.

Don't' get me started about cats. Why they ever were created is a mystery to me. Their view point is ridiculous and they are sneaky. I can't even tell you how many there are! It seems as if they are everywhere. Over time I have learned to deal with them. They still steal my food while often messing up my pillow on the couch. You have to watch them all the time. Why does my April love cats so much? They are warm and fuzzy yes, but that's where the cuteness stops and the diabolical conniving begins.

The only other animal as smart as me is the bird Tutu. He and I have come to an agreement to co-exist peacefully.

There are big tortoises outside who really don't speak dog very well. I try to avoid them when I go outside. They don't listen and will stomp right over you if you get in the way.

One thing I did notice about them is that their poop is gigantic. Really different than most I've seen. Are they here on this planet to learn things too? Gosh I can't imagine what they would want to learn. All they really seem to care about is eating. So dear Universe, take care of them. I think they are distracted by all the food my April gives to them. I think they got off course in their quest for growth or something.

The peacocks and the pheasants don't like me very much. Once I snuck into their cage when my April wasn't looking. They ignored me completely until I started to bark at them. I was only trying to teach them how to behave. Apparently they were offended by me. They flew up off the ground and honked at me until my April came running out to get me. She was pretty mad at me but it wasn't my fault that my magnificent presence upset them.

Any ways.

I was on restriction after that caper. Last but not least is the little intruder who has become like a kid sister to me. We get along because she knows who is boss!..... ME! Here name is Little Bit, however there is really nothing little about her. Her mom was very sick and went to you dear Universe, which left her all alone. My April brought her home against my wishes. I admit I was not very welcoming at first because I thought she would take away from my sweet set up. You were right again dear Universe, she added to it instead. She has lived with us now for quite a few years. We get along because she knows I am the boss!

I don't think she steals my treats but sometimes I am not sure. One time I knew I had my cookie. I had run to the window to tell off a squirrel who had the nerve to eat his nut right there, making a huge mess. By the time I got back to where my cookie was, it was gone.

I looked everywhere but no luck. Little Bit had been sitting there the whole time. I asked her if she had seen my cookie but she said she didn't know what I was talking about. She looked at me with her little eyes with great respect and sincerity. Of course then I believed her.

Then.....

While I was still searching I saw Bit get up out of the corner of my eye. Underneath her was my cookie! Oh boy! Was I ever mad!

When she saw she was caught she quickly gobbled my whole cookie down her greedy throat. "I don't know what you are talking about!" she cried.

I ran to my April who promptly gave me another cookie.

BUT!

What about the little thief?! I know. I know dear Universe, she had had a rough time when her mom died but that doesn't give her permission to steal, does it?

Oh.

Ok.

I get it. Little Bit is reacting to her loss by comforting herself with my cookie?

Anyways.....

Little Bit has learned not to steal my cookies over time. It's because she now realizes there are plenty of cookies. The cats tell me she is still a thief but I have a little more patience now.

My April continues to be the love of my life. I stay by her side constantly.

She needs me.

I need her more.

I feel myself blending with her all the time. Without this relationship I would be so sad.

My only regret is that Blade never got to experience all this love. Maybe when I see him where you are at dear Universe, I can talk him into going back into physical reality to be with my April again.

I'm curled up on my fluffy dog bed right now. My April is doing her spirit work. I close my eyes and blend with her. It's so special and so cool. I have a lot more adventures to play in before I see you again dear Universe. Maybe I will write more about my adventures in a while. Right now I feel complete. The world is not such a bad place after all.

I will try to help all puppies find their comfortable place. The key to that is finding your human. I believe that now.

What's that dear Universe? You want me to do what?

Oh Ok.

Sure, I can do that.

I will continue to speak my mind about the earth and the people in it. Sometimes humans move too fast and lose their spiritual perspective. You and I together can help them.

Ok.

Cool.

A puppy's perspective is sometimes more clear. I will share my inner knowing. I will keep my whiskers focused upon good things and share them.

It's going to be a lot of fun and continued growth.

I'm all about that.

***

About The Author

April Crawford is a pet and animal lover. She lives in Southern California with the many animals who are members of the family.

(This picture was taken by "Maha" in Maine, USA.)